LIKE FRESH BREAD

Sunday Homilies in the Parish

ROBERT P. WAZNAK, S.S.

To THE PREACHER,
WHOM GOD PREPARED,
Go GET'EM MAN!
(VIRGIL)

For I am
with Best Wishes!
Robert P Waznak M

PAULIST PRESS
New York/Mahwah

Library of Congress Cataloging-in-Publication Data

Waznak, Robert P.
    Like fresh bread: Sunday homilies in the parish/by Robert P. Waznak.
        p. cm.
    Includes bibliographical references.
    ISBN 0-8091-3378-4 (paper)
    1. Sermons, Catholic. 2 Sermons, American. I. Title.
BX1756.W38L55 1993
252′.02—dc20   93-2695
                                                                               CIP

Published by Paulist Press
997 Macarthur Boulevard
Mahwah, NJ 07430

Printed and bound in the
United States of America

TABLE OF CONTENTS

CHRISTMAS

LENT

EASTER

ORDINARY TIME

FEASTS

En Memoria
de mi hermano

Francisco P. Roig Vilella

PREFACE

I spend most of my week struggling to teach others how to preach. When Sunday comes, I have an opportunity not only to preach but to practice what I teach. When the homilies in this book were first created, I did not intend them for publication, but for proclamation. But in the past few years, students in preaching classes and participants in preaching workshops began to ask for examples of what and how I preached on Sundays. Their requests were certainly fair. Many speakers and authors lament the "sad state of preaching" in our time and propose a homiletic overhaul, yet few (especially Catholic authors) have been willing to offer models of what that overhaul would look like. Thus, the idea of this collection sprang from my experience as both homiletician and homilist.

The title for this book came from a story I heard while on sabbatical one summer in Brazil. I was conversing one day with Anna Flora Anderson and Gilberto Gorgulho, O.P. who team-teach sacred scripture at the seminary in the archdiocese of São Paulo. Father Gorgulho is a scholarly professor and a popular preacher. Anna Flora is a vivacious teacher who is always searching for the ripe image. She urged her colleague to tell me about her favorite image of the liturgical homily. Gilberto spoke about how central a loaf of fresh bread is on the Brazilian table. "A homily," he said, "is like fresh bread." He then went on to say how many preachers do not feed people with fresh bread because they have given up the prayerful task of reading the signs of the times in light of the biblical text of the day; "they serve stale bread." Gilberto told me, "No doubt, you have noticed how creative we are here in reconstructing the bread that was once fresh—we toast it, we put fruit and sweets on it, we make croutons out of it for our chicken soup and sprinkle its crumbs on our

1

fried bananas. There comes a time, however, that no matter how well we toast the bread or even dunk it into our rich black coffee, the bread just won't go down the throat. The bread is stale. It is time to bake fresh bread!"

With the reforms of Vatican II came the biblical homily—fresh bread for the table of the Lord. In *Sunday After Sunday: Preaching the Homily as Story*,[1] I proposed that an ideal liturgical homily should contain three stories: the story of the preacher, the story of God, and the story of the listener. This proposal was influenced by the homiletic reforms of the Second Vatican Council and the realities of our times.

The Story of the Preacher. The key to the renewal of the homily by Vatican II is a renewal of the homilist. God's living word is spoken through human words which emerge not just from study, but from the preacher's prayerful interpretation of human experience. By the story of the preacher, I am not referring to the dreadful act of navel-gazing where the preacher's narcissism chokes out any chance of God's story to take root. I am speaking in the contemporary context of personal witness. Paul VI put it this way, "Modern man listens more willingly to witnesses than to teachers and if he does listen to teachers, it is because they are witnesses."[2] I do not suggest that in every homily the preacher explicitly share a personal anecdote. As I understand the story of the preacher, it means that the homily emerges not primarily from a book (biblical commentary, homily service, church document, newspaper account), but from the preacher's own religious imagination and prayer. I am speaking in the tradition of Thomas Aquinas who believed that preachers are called "to share with others the fruit of their contemplation." The preacher must learn how to tell his or her story appropriately so that it intersects with the listeners' experience and the challenge and hope of the gospel.[3]

The 1982 document on preaching produced by the National Council of Catholic Bishops, *Fulfilled in Your Hearing: The Homily in the Sunday Assembly,* emphasizes:

> Ultimately, that's what preaching is all about, not lofty theological speculation, not painstaking biblical exegesis, not oratorical flamboyance. The preacher is a person speaking to people about life and faith.[4]

A preacher is sometimes an exegete, sometimes a teacher, but primarily a poet, which was the favorite metaphor for the preacher that Karl Rahner used a quarter of a century ago.[5] Preaching is information, but it is much more than that. It is the moving of hearts, an invitation to conversion, the sharing of a new vision through God's living word. Robert Frost defined poetry as "a way of grappling with life."[6] Preachers who ignore their own grappling with life can hardly touch the lives of others. Scripture scholar Walter Brueggemann writes:

> The new conversation, on which our very lives depend, requires a poet and not a moralist. . . . The deep places in our lives—places of resistance and embrace—are not ultimately reached by instruction [but by] images, metaphors, and phrases that line out the world differently apart from our fear and hurt. The reflection that comes from the poet requires playfulness, imagination, and interpretation.[7]

The Story of God. Vatican II's renewal of the liturgical homily signaled a return to the proclamation of the story of God: "All the preaching of the church . . . should be nourished and ruled by sacred scripture" (*Dei Verbum,* no. 21). The reformers of Vatican II revived the ancient tradition of preaching which flowed directly from the biblical readings and liturgical celebration of the day and led to the celebration of the sacraments.

At the same time that Vatican II was insisting on biblical preaching, scholars were publishing new biblical commentaries. Supply met demand. A popular homiletic method that followed the council concentrated on applying the insights of historical-critical study of the sacred texts to preaching. But many preachers soon learned that it was not enough for the preacher to search out the authenticity of a particular text: Was there a star over Bethlehem? Did Jesus walk on water? Was Mary in the upper room at Pentecost? When preachers approach the scriptures *only* with questions of authenticity in mind, they miss the symbolic, evocative, existential perception of the text. They forget the church's worthy tradition of *lectio divina.* They neglect their poetic vocation of trusting in what Paul Ricoeur has called "the second naiveté." They fail to grasp the fact that the biblical text is fulfilled in our hearing.

The historical-critical method still provides necessary and helpful parameters for constructing a convincing homily. Besides the historical-critical, today's homilists are discovering other biblical methods of interpretation, e.g. literary, sociological, canonical, feminist, and liberation criticism to assist them in their homiletic task.

Recent homiletic literature encourages not so much an explanation of scripture with an application to life, but an interpretation of life *in light of* the scriptures. *Fulfilled in Your Hearing* speaks of "a scriptural interpretation of human existence which enables a community to recognize God's active presence."[8] In the homily, "the preacher does not so much attempt to explain the Scriptures as to interpret the human situation through the Scriptures."[9] The NCCB document extended the restrictive definitions of the homily found in *Sacrosanctum Concilium*. It assimilated the "reading of the signs of the times" motif from *Gaudium et Spes* and insights from contemporary biblical and theological studies. *Fulfilled in Your Hearing* also reflected the biblical hermeneutic found in the last chapter of *Dei Verbum*. That hermeneutic includes both reason and faith. Reason seeks to grasp the meaning of the text; faith leads to being grasped *by* the meaning of the text.

The new shift, from an interpretation of scripture with an application to life, to an interpretation of the human situation through scripture, helps the homilist to name grace not only in the liturgy, but in our world of boundaries and limitations. *Fulfilled in Your Hearing* names the homilist not a teacher but a "mediator of meaning."[10] As "mediator of meaning," the homilist strives to attend to the present moment as revelatory of God.

The Story of the Listener. Karl Rahner's foundational statement that God's self-communication is human transcendence and vice versa helps us to situate the context of liturgical preaching in the transcendental experience of men and women.[11] Recent Catholic theological literature on preaching highlights the concrete experiences of people. It is a theology of preaching that is incarnational and sacramental. It is anchored in God's word in history and in human experience, naming grace in our world of limitations. Systematic theologians are urging a contemporary mystagogy which can enable people to surrender to mystery found in the midst of ordinary daily life.[12]

On most Sundays I preach at Good Shepherd Parish, Mount Vernon, Virginia, located in the diocese of Arlington. The boundaries of the parish encompass the historic Mount Vernon estate and most of George Washington's farms, including River Farm to the north and Mansion Farm on the south. The Potomac River forms the eastern border and the historic black community of Gum Springs is on the west, bounded by U.S. Route 1. Good Shepherd is comprised of 1,622 families. The people are a mix of upper middle-class, middle-class and those in public housing. Salvadoran and Nicaraguan refugee families sit next to Pentagon officials and old Virginia stock at Sunday eucharist. Good Shepherd Parish was formed in 1965, the same year that the Second Vatican Council urged homilists not to preach "in a general and abstract way," but to relate "the gospel to the concrete circumstances of life" (*Presbyterorum Ordinis*, no. 4).

Many of the concrete circumstances of life found in these homilies are local because I believe that our preaching must value the assembly's particular issues, events, seasons, characters, questions, addictions, struggles, and blessings. The *Instruction* that sought to implement the liturgical reforms of Vatican II spoke about preaching that attends to the "peculiar needs of the congregation."[13] Our preaching must attend to the *sensus* and the *tempus fidelium*. That is what the writers of the gospels did: they told the story of Christ's paschal mystery in the unique context of the story of their listeners. Canonical critics remind us that the stories of scripture were remembered and "canonized" because they told people about their lives, and at the same time told them there was something more. There was an alternative way of looking at their lives and their world—God's way.

Like the poets, the sacred writers paid attention to detail. Jesus was not just asleep in a boat tossed by the waves of a storm, he was cuddled up on a cushion (Mark 4:38); the younger son was not just "down and out" but he worked on a farm where he fed pigs and was so hungry that he longed to eat the pigs' leftovers (Luke 15:15–16); Paul quoted an early Christian hymn about Christ's obedience to death but he added a significant and embarrassing detail about that death: it was death *on a cross* (Philippians 2:8). Preachers must take notice of the concrete circumstances and the specific details in the biblical text and context of their listeners. Once again, preachers can learn from poets, artists, and visionaries like architect Mïes van der Rohe who once said that "God hides in the details."

This collection of homilies contains concrete details that are peculiar to the time and place where they were first preached. Whenever possible, I have deleted local references in order to appeal to readers who live outside the Washington Beltway. Some of the homilies include references to current events that are already dated. I have kept these in order to preserve the structural integrity of the particular homily and the spirit in which it was first preached.

Although these homilies were preached in a particular time and place to a unique congregation, they hopefully represent the concerns, dreams and struggles of all who come to the eucharist with a common faith in Jesus Christ. There is a sense in which the people of Good Shepherd Parish in Mount Vernon, Virginia are like all Christian communities. As *Fulfilled in Your Hearing* reminds us:

> Like humans everywhere, the people who make up the liturgical assembly are people hungry, sometimes desperately so, for meaning in their lives. . . . Without ultimate meaning, we are ultimately unsatisfied. If we hear a word which gives our lives another level of meaning, which interprets them in relation to God, then our response is to turn to this source of meaning in an attitude of praise and thanksgiving.[14]

A Weaving of Stories. I believe that an ideal liturgical homily, as envisioned by the homiletic reforms of Vatican II and developed in our own times, is a weaving of the stories of preacher, God, and listener. I am not suggesting that each homily contain $33\frac{1}{3}$ percent of each story. The three-story model that I have described is meant to serve as a grid by which we can prepare and evaluate our preaching.

A Narrative Form. Although Vatican II proposed a new vision of the liturgical homily, it offered no new models for the form of that homily. Post-conciliar documents speak of the homily's form only in generic ways: the homily should be preached "in a way that is suited to the community's capacity and way of life that is relevant to the circumstances of the celebration."[15] "It [the homily] should be neither too long nor too short."[16]

In recent years homiletic literature on the subject of the sermon's form has flourished.[17] Many "narrative homileticians" have urged preachers to shape their homilies not like lawyers' briefs (deductive, propositional, syllogistic), but like stories. They have encouraged preachers to concentrate on the narrative discourse of scripture. Narrative homileticians have debunked the old homiletic method that forced an Aristotelian straitjacket onto a biblical story. They have argued for preachers to appreciate biblical texts as literature in their own right. Just as the biblical narratives had a power to disclose a living meaning, a poetic alternative, a fresh way of "reading the signs of the times," so preaching that is formed in the shape of a narrative has the same evocative potential.

Narrative preaching does not mean preaching that weaves in and out like a stream-of-consciousness. Narrative preaching is preaching that moves like a story. Narrative preaching does not necessarily mean that the homily is chock-full of stories. Eugene Lowry sees a narrative sermon as a pattern of development that may or may not contain a single story. Lowry compares this way of preaching to the model Aristotle presents in *Poetics:* The narrative sermon "moves from opening disequilibrium (or conflict) through escalation (complication) to surprising reversal (*peripetia*) into closing denouement."[18] The homilies in this collection represent my own brand of narrative preaching. They appear here as I first typed them—as a preacher's script, not in grammatical paragraphs but in an oral form of communication.

There are many local angels who have hovered over this collection with support and friendly advice. I am grateful to the people of Good Shepherd Parish who have challenged and nurtured me in Christian community; the academic dean of the Washington Theological Union, James A. Coriden, and my colleague, James A. Wallace, C.Ss.R., for their encouragement and helpful suggestions; my editor, Lawrence Boadt, C.S.P., for his keen advice, and to Michael J. Gallagher of Trinity College and Anita Joseph Reeves, C.S.C. for their special assistance in helping me to prepare this collection.

Feast of Pentecost, 1992

Notes

1. Robert P. Waznak, *Sunday After Sunday: Preaching the Homily as Story* (New York: Paulist, 1983).

2. Pope Paul VI, "Address to the Members of the *Consilium de Laicis*" (October 2, 1974): *AAS* 66 (1974) p. 568.

3. For a balanced treatment of this topic, see Richard L. Thulin, *The "I" of the Sermon* (Minneapolis: Fortress, 1989).

4. National Conference of Catholic Bishops, *Fulfilled in Your Hearing: The Homily in the Sunday Assembly* (Washington, DC: United States Conference, 1982).

5. Karl Rahner, "Priest and Poet," *The Word: Readings in Theology* (New York: P.J. Kenedy and Sons, 1964) pp. 3–26.

6. Edward Connery Laterm, ed., *Interviews with Robert Frost* (New York: Holt, Rinehart and Winston, 1966) p. 58.

7. Walter Brueggemann, *Finally Comes the Poet: Daring Speech for Proclamation* (Minneapolis: Fortress Press, 1989) pp. 109–110.

8. *Fulfilled in Your Hearing*, p. 29.

9. Ibid. p. 20.

10. Ibid. p. 7.

11. Karl Rahner, *Theological Investigations*, translated by David Bourke (New York: Crossroad, 1982) Vol. 11, p. 28.

12. See Eileen A. McKeown, *A Theology of the Proclamation Based on Karl Rahner's Theology of the Word* (Fordham University, 1989) Ph.D. theology dissertation, and Mary Catherine Hilkert, *Towards a Theology of Proclamation: Edward Schille-*

beeckx's Hermeneutics as a Foundation for a Theology of Proclamation (The Catholic University of America, 1984) Ph.D. theology dissertation.

13. *"Inter Oecumenici,"* 26 September 1964, 54.

14. *Fulfilled in Your Hearing,* p. 7.

15. *Eucharistiae Participationem,* 27 April 1972, 15.

16. *Catechesi Tradendae,* 16 October 1979, 48.

17. For a review of the literature on narrative preaching, see Robert P. Waznak, "Like a Story: An Update on Narrative Preaching," *New Theology Review,* Vol. 4, no. 2, May 1991, pp. 93–100.

18. Eugene Lowry, "The Difference Between Story Preaching and Narrative Preaching." Paper presented at the Academy of Homiletics Meeting, December 1988, Drew University.

ADVENT

1
ADVENT'S ANXIETY
Second Sunday of Advent (A)

- Isaiah 11:1–10
- Romans 15:4–9
- Matthew 3:1–12

(Liturgically speaking, Advent has nothing to do with Christmas trees. But in real life, this is the Sunday when many of the people will purchase their Christmas trees. As was mentioned in the Preface, the liturgical calendar and the people's calendar are not necessarily synchronized. In this homily I tried to speak about what people were doing and experiencing that Sunday *in light of* the scriptures of Advent.)

In the old days, artificial trees were made of aluminum,
    a strange imitation of nature's lovely evergreens.
When I was a kid, a cynical cousin announced to his parents
    who had just finished decorating
    an artificial aluminum tree,
    "How beautiful! I love the smell of aluminum!"
You don't see aluminum Christmas trees these days.
Technology has perfected the art
    so that artificial trees look awfully convincing.
Add a healthy spray of "Scent of Noel"
    and you could fool even my cynical cousin.

I read a newspaper report the other day saying that
    one-third of all the Christmas trees
    bought in the U.S.A. this year will be artificial.
I wonder what that statistic means.
Does it mean that one-third of our nation
    is really attracted to the *untree*?
Or does it mean that only two-thirds of the people dare to venture

into one of the most anxious places of this season—
   the Christmas tree lot?

If you want to capture the pulse of this season,
   go to the place where balsams, firs and pines
   stand ready for inspection.
Listen to the anxious people as they search for
   the perfect tree.
Since I belong to the courageous two-thirds of the people,
   here's a conversation I heard the other day at a tree lot:
      "Here's a nice one," said an optimistic fellow.
      "Look, except for this little space right here,
         it's a pretty tree."
      "Little space? Are you kidding?" asked his wife.
      "The tree is ugly.
      That space is one foot long."
      "That's OK; once we get the ornaments on,
         it will be just fine."
      "Ornaments? But we don't have an ornament one foot long!"

There are other spots besides the Christmas tree lot
   where anxiety reigns supreme this time of year:
   Toys-R-Us on a Saturday morning;
   the highway on a snowy Friday afternoon;
   the office party on a Tuesday night.
Like the Christmas tree lot,
   these places are filled with people
   who are anxious because they want
   the perfect tree,
   the perfect gift,
   the perfectly good time.
The media fuel the flames of a perfect Christmas
   with flashing images not only of perfect trees,
   but of perfectly baked cookies.
Even the snow that Madison Avenue produces for its ads
   looks perfect.
In our commercials,
   everyone looks happy and satisfied with the gifts.
The anxiety mounts.
We want our pre-Christmas and our Christmas to be like that—
   perfect!

On this Second Sunday of Advent,
    the church sheds a spot light on a very anxious person,
    John the Baptist.
He was anxious because he also sought the perfect solution
    to all of the problems of his time.
He was so anxious,
    he didn't even take out time
    to buy his clothes from the department store
    or his food from the supermarket.
He wore the skin of animals
    and ate food that would shock
    even today's natural food fanatics.
John the Baptist would have been holy terror
    in the Christmas tree lot.
He would have thrown every tree that wasn't perfect
    into the fire.
John was anxious because he too was into perfection.
He wanted to prepare the people
    for a Messiah who would make all things
    perfect on this earth.
John believed that the Messiah would settle things
    once and for all!
He would stamp out all the imperfect people in the world
    and make things right.
John's favorite word was *reform.*
    "Change your minds and your hearts
    because the reign of God
    that people have waited so long for
    will soon be here," he proclaimed.
But when the Messiah finally came,
    he wasn't what John had expected.
Instead of a stern judge who would clean house,
    Jesus preached a gospel of forgiveness.
Instead of a Messiah of fire and brimstone,
    Jesus was a man of peace and love.
Instead of coming only for the perfect,
    Jesus said that he had come for
    the imperfect.
To John's credit,
    John the Baptist practiced what he preached.
He reformed his own life,
    and accepted Jesus as he was.

This Christmas, like all Christmases,
   will not be perfect.
Small things will get in the way.
There will be a burnt-out bulb on a string of lights,
   a couple of burnt cookies in the batch,
   a co-worker who will get too happy at the office party,
   a kid who will get a neater gift than you,
   a loony relative who will make an impossible demand on you.
We will get anxious
   and we will be tempted to grab our winnowing-fans
   and blow all of these imperfections away.
When these anxious moments come our way
   let's try to listen to the herald's voice
   crying out in the desert.
Let's try to reform not others,
   but our own lives.
Such a message will keep things in perspective
   and change our anxiety into hope.
We are not preparing for a perfect Christmas,
   but for a perfect Christ who is mightier
   than all our dreams.

2
DOES SNOOPY BREAK TRADITION?
Fourth Sunday of Advent (A)

- Isaiah 7:10–14
- Romans 1:1–7
- Matthew 1:18–24

There's something about this season that stirs up old stories.
When I prayed over this gospel story of Joseph's dream,
I remembered what happened one Christmas
   when I lived in Baltimore.
Each Sunday I used to celebrate the two afternoon masses
   at the old basilica in the city.
The basilica is the oldest cathedral in the United States.
It is a stately masterpiece designed by Latrobe,
   the architect who designed our nation's Capitol building.
Many worshipers feel at home in the old basilica
   because it looks and smells like a church from the past.
The basilica is a temple of religious tradition.

A serious threat to the basilica's tradition
   came one year a few days before Christmas.
When I arrived for the four P.M. mass,
   the sacristan immediately greeted me
   with the startling news:
   someone had put Snoopy in the nativity scene!
Some people, for whom tradition was a badge of Catholicism,
   wanted Snoopy out of the manger.
Other parishioners, however, were delighted with
   the new visitor in the crib.
In fact, word was getting around Baltimore about
   Snoopy and the baby Jesus.

15

The sacristan told me that many parents were beginning to bring
  their kids to see
  the *new* nativity in the old basilica.
As I knelt at the crib with the pastor, Monsignor Love,
  even my middle-aged cynicism was shaken.
There, in the midst of Mary, Joseph, Jesus and the shepherds
  dressed in traditional Florentine clothes,
  was a stuffed Snoopy doll.
Nobody knew who put Snoopy in the crib.
Our best guess was that a child simply wanted
  to give God her favorite toy.
For that reason, Monsignor Love declared, despite tradition,
  Snoopy stays;
  Snoopy belongs.

I'd like to think the one most happy
  to welcome Snoopy into the crèche was Joseph,
  the one whom the gospel calls "just."
When faced with the dilemma of Mary's pregnancy,
  Joseph breaks with tradition and adopts Jesus.
Joseph gives to Jesus what we all look for in life,
  a name, a home, a family,
  a sense of belonging.
In adopting Jesus as his own child,
  Joseph follows the example of the just God we find
  throughout the Bible:
  a just God who always adopts
  the most helpless victims in the world—
  orphans.
Orphans are those people who have no rights,
  no voice in government,
  no representation in the court.
The good news of the Bible is that God adopts orphans
  and gives them a name,
  a new identity and a new belonging.
God assures all orphans that despite their plight,
  their God is Emmanuel, God with us!

Toward the end of this remarkable year of 1989
  there will be a good deal of speculation about why
  the nations of Eastern and Central Europe
  in rapid succession

began to tumble the walls and kick out the dictators
    who for so long had denied them their human rights.
Some will say it was the *perestroika* of Gorbachev,
    or the military resolve of Reagan,
    or the failure of communism as a viable economic system.
Who knows?
Could it be that the real reason for this renaissance of freedom
    is found only when we let our four Advent candles
    shed light on the people and events of our time?
We are an Advent people "who mourn in lonely exile here."
There is something about people that longs to belong,
    that wants a name and an identity.

The first questions put to us as little children are:
    What's your name?
    Where do you live?
    What do you want to be when you grow up?
These are the questions with which we begin
    our journey of identity.

The totalitarian regimes that have dominated
    Eastern and Central Europe since World War II
    had robbed the people of that sense of
    individual identity.
There was only one place
    where people could feel that they belonged—
    the church.
Often the gospel was preached in a hushed voice
    in underground churches,
    but it was preached.
And, thank God, this good news finally broke through
    the barbed wire.
It is the same good news we heard proclaimed this morning:
That despite our traps and dilemmas,
    we have nothing to fear
    because our God has not left us orphans.
We have a name:
    we are *children of God.*
And God has a name.
It is *Emmanuel,*
    God is with us!

I don't know if Snoopy still snuggles with the cattle
  in the basilica's crèche.
I'd like to think he does.
I'd like to think he still belongs.
After all, this is the season when we dream about the day
  when the lion will lie down with the lamb.
So why not Snoopy?
What I do know is that if we really want to capture
  the true spirit of Christmas this year,
    we could take a clue from the just man Joseph
    and give someone a name,
    a sense of dignity,
    a sense of belonging.
You, too, have the grace and the power to make someone
  a child of God.

3
PLANTING BULBS IN ADVENT
First Sunday of Advent (B)

* Isaiah 63:16–17,19; 64:2–7
* 1 Corinthians 1:3–9
* Mark 13:33–37

When I was a little boy, the word "Advent" frightened me.
It was because of what happened
   to my cousin Johnny and me at the movies.
Johnny's dad was a Seventh-Day Adventist
   who lived his religion to the hilt.
Since my Aunt Ann, my Cousin Johnny and his sister Judy were
     Catholics,
   they would spend every Saturday at our house
   while my Uncle John spent his sabbath in church
   and out on the road searching for converts.
This arrangement suited me just fine because of the buddy I had
   in my cousin Johnny.
Every Saturday we would play, scheme, fight and make up.
It was a perfect relationship until one snowy Saturday afternoon
   when we went to the movies.

I had to convince Johnny to go to the movies
   since his father had grave misgivings about wasting time
   on entertainment,
   especially on a Saturday.
Adventists take the message of today's scripture readings
   quite literally.
They really believe and hope for Christ's second coming.
They meditate on the prophet Isaiah who prayed:
   "Would that you might meet us doing right,
   that we were mindful of you in our ways!"

19

Sitting in a movie theater on a Saturday afternoon
   was not exactly considered doing the right thing
   even if it was a Walt Disney double feature.

When my cousin and I came out of the theater
   we were surprised not only by a snowstorm
   but by Uncle John who was waiting for us in his Packard.
Because of the storm,
   he had returned to our house earlier than expected.
When he found out that his son and wayward nephew
   were at the movies,
   he drove to the theater to pick us up.
To make matters even worse,
   the workmen at the theater
   had already changed the movie title on the marquee.
I don't remember what the new title was,
   but it definitely wasn't Disney!
As Ricky Ricardo used to say to Lucy,
   we had "a lot of *splanin* to do" to my uncle.

It wasn't till years later, when I was in the seminary,
   that I began to understand
   why certain Christian denominations,
   like Seventh-Day Adventists and Pentecostals,
   take the idea of Christ's second coming so seriously.
These religious groups find rooted in the Bible
   an eagerness,
   even an ecstasy about
   the coming of God into their world.

Even after "the Word was made flesh,"
   there was a profound expectancy
   for the second coming of the Word.
St. Paul, today, speaks of waiting for
   the full revelation of the Lord.
The disciples of Jesus really believed they were
   doorkeepers
   and that at any minute their master would return.
They believed that the second coming
   would happen in their lifetime.
But with the passage of centuries,
   Christians begin to settle in and forget about

Christ's second coming.
Of course, the church still had the season of Advent,
    but it became a kind of "let's pretend time."
Let's pretend that we live in that period of time
    before the birth of Jesus
    when women and men longed for the coming of the Messiah,
    when they dreamed dreams and sang songs about
    a wonderful day when swords would be beaten into plowshares,
    when the lion would lie down with the lamb,
    when a fresh shoot would sprout forth from the stump of Jesse,
    when a virgin would bear a son and name him Emmanuel.
Advent became a season of commemorating the time
    before the birth of Jesus
    instead of a season of expecting that
    Jesus was going to come again.

Just as my Uncle John nudged us Catholics to take seriously
    the second coming of the Lord,
    the liturgy nudges us today with scriptures
    about Christ's second coming.
We began our First Sunday of Advent not just as a time
    to commemorate Christ's first coming at Christmas
    but as a special time to remember that he is coming again.
God is coming again to save all people.
As the gospel parable reminds us today,
    we don't know *when* it will happen
    but that it *will* happen.

This is the meaning of Advent,
    a deep trust that despite our pre-Christmas rush
    and anxieties,
    despite the gloomy prospects of war in the Middle East,
    despite all our fears and lost hopes,
    God is coming to save all people.

On the way to school the other day,
    I saw something that sparked my Advent hope.
As I drove past an elementary school,
    I saw a teacher with her small band of kids.
The teacher wasn't helping them to put up Christmas lights
    or a Santa Claus display.
She was teaching them how to dig into the near frozen ground

and plant tiny bulbs for the coming of spring.
She was teaching them to hope against hope.
She was teaching them something about expecting promises
    to be fulfilled.
That teacher is like the church
    helping us to dig deeper into the meaning of our faith;
    nudging us to take time during this anxious season
    to plant some seeds of hope in our God
    who is coming to save all people.

Every now and then I hear someone say,
    "I just can't get into the Christmas spirit."
Maybe that's because we have never entered the Advent spirit.
Advent is not a time to tremble in fear
    but to wait in joy.
Advent is not a time to give up
    but to begin anew.
"Rejoice, rejoice,
    to you shall come Emmanuel."

4
DARE TO BE DIFFERENT
Third Sunday of Advent (B)

- Isaiah 61:1–2,10–11
- 1 Thessalonians 5:16–24
- John 1:6–8,19–28

During this time of year, television begins to challenge
   the cynical with the magical.
Old reruns of sentimental favorites like
   A Christmas Carol, and *Miracle on 34th Street,*
   Peter Pan, and *The Wizard of Oz* compete with
   Roseanne and *Who's the Boss?*
At the heart of all these films are children
   who melt a Scrooge's heart
   because they give a whole new perspective on life.
These kids are a refreshing relief
   from the wise brats of today's TV shows.
Their wisdom stems not from acting like little adults,
   but from the lovely innocence of childhood.

Last Monday night NBC aired a show called "The Dreamer of Oz,"
   which told the story of L. Frank Baum
   who wrote the classic tale about the innocence and wisdom
   of a girl named Dorothy.
Baum was a dreamer because he wanted to write
   an American fairy tale that was different;
   a fairy tale that didn't scare kids to death
   or hit them over the head with a frightening moral.
Instead, the story ends with Dorothy's simple discovery that the
   Wizard of Oz
   is no more a wizard than she,
   the Scarecrow, the Tin Man and the Lion.

But before Dorothy learns that simple lesson,
   she dares to cry out to the Wizard of Oz,
   "You're a very bad man!"
But even the phony wizard
   makes a wonderful discovery about himself.
He says, "No, Dorothy, I'm a very good man
   but a very bad wizard!"

A major actor in our Advent story is a man
   who many thought was a wizard.
Thousands went off to see the strange prophet
   who preached and baptized
   in the wilderness around the Dead Sea.
John ate, dressed and preached
   like no other man they had ever known.
He was a man who dared to be different.
The road that the pilgrims followed to get to John
   was no yellow brick road.
The road was a dusty, bumpy trail.
The only time that roads were ever
   smoothed and straightened in those days
   was when a king or conqueror was planning
   to visit his territory.
Because John the Baptist believed strongly
   that the king of heaven
   was about to come into his territory,
   he told the people to "make straight the way of the Lord!"

John was such a wizard in convincing the people
   that the Messiah was near
   that even the cardinals and archbishops of his day
   were curious.
And so they sent some monsignors to question the prophet.
What is curious about John's response is that
   he answers in the negative.
He tells these religious leaders who he is not:
   "I am *not* the Messiah."
He also says that he is not Elijah,
   nor a prophet returned from the dead.
He tells them that he is not a wizard
   but simply a voice crying out in the desert,
   daring to be different,

daring to tell them that the Messiah
  was already in their midst.

It isn't easy to dare to be *different*
  especially in this season of anxious preparation.
There are powerful consumer forces
  that convince us to be *the same.*
We need to have the toy, the perfume, the gadget
  that the newspaper and TV ads tell us *everybody*
  is going to get this Christmas.

That is why, here at our Good Shepherd community,
  we chose as our Advent theme:
  "In joy and simplicity we bring gifts to the One who comes."
We dare to be different.
We dare to live in joy
  despite the many concrete signs of sadness that surround us.
We dare to embrace simplicity
  when so many complicated demands are made on us.
We dare not only to give gifts for those who have little.
We give gifts to the One who comes
  in the poor and the needy in our midst.

The Jesse Tree in the narthex highlights
  the needs of many in our surrounding community:
  postage stamps for prisoners,
  food for United Community Ministry's pantry,
  toys and other gifts for low-income families,
  toiletries and small gifts for shelter residents,
  ornaments for next year's Christmas
  at a senior health care center,
  and baby clothes for
  Children and Family Services of Catholic Charities.

The Jesse Tree is different
  from other trees we see this time of year.
It is decorated with gifts not for those who have,
  but for those who need.

The story of John the Baptist that we heard today
  tells of a man who dared to tell others
  that he was not a wizard

but a man who was preparing
for the coming of the wisest of them all.
John is a good model for us this season
to dare to be different.

To dare to be different in the mall,
at the office party,
on the freeway,
with our neighbors, our friends, our families, strangers.
To dare in joy and simplicity
to bring our gifts
to the One who comes!

5
MARY'S WAITING AND LETTING GO
Fourth Sunday of Advent (B)

- 2 Samuel 7:1–5,8–11,16
- Romans 16:25–27
- Luke 1:26–38

The season of Advent isn't easy for a people
   who have a short waiting span.
Kids can't wait until their Christmas gifts are ripped open.
Department stores advertise sales
   as if Christmas is already over.
Many people can't seem to wait until
   the sanctions against Iraq finally work.
The Soviets and the new democracies in Eastern Europe
   are getting testy because the fruits of *glasnost* still seem
   like cabbage in the sky.

We've just lit our fourth Advent candle,
   but already there are commentaries
   about who will be *Time* magazine's "Person of the Year."
Bart Simpson and Sadam Hussein seem to be this year's favorites.
And even though there are still
   nine more years until the year 2000,
   nominees are already coming into *Time* for
   "The Person of the Twentieth Century."
Imagine what would have happened
   if there had been a *Time* magazine in 1490
   and the experts had already chosen
   "The Person of the Fifteenth Century."
Christopher Columbus never would have had a chance!
There's something foolish about not waiting,

about not giving peace a chance,
about not waiting to open our gifts until Christmas.

Political analyst and baseball buff George Will
    can't seem to wait.
He already has his short list
    for "The Person of the Millennium,"
    which includes
    Machiavelli, Luther, Washington, Jefferson, and Lincoln.
Some have expressed surprise that Jackie Robinson or Babe Ruth
    didn't make Will's list.
Others have noted how his choices display a bias
    for political figures
    rather than scientists and artists.
Some have also noticed how
    decidedly provincial were his candidates:
    three American presidents,
    two from Virginia.

I often tell my student preachers that they are supposed to read the
    newspaper
    with the haunting images and visions
    of the Sunday scriptures
    still dancing in their heads and hearts.
When I tried to follow my own advice this week,
    I was struck with how the angel Gabriel's
    annunciation to virgin Mary
    contrasts with how we choose
    "The Person of the Year" or "the Millennium."
Once again,
    God's ways are not our ways.
And God's messengers seem to have a different message
    than today's media messengers.

To appreciate just how revolutionary
    Gabriel's annunciation to Mary was,
    it's important to remember that
    just before he made a call on Mary
    he also brought a message to the future father of
    John the Baptist.
The contrast between the two annunciations is quite revealing.
The first takes place in the great city of Jerusalem

to the priest Zechariah.
Gabriel then takes a shuttle flight to Nazareth
    for his second annunciation.
The archangel appears not in a temple of a great city
    but in a humble home in a little town.
He brings a heavenly message
    not to a man in the powerful office of priest,
    but to a teenage girl who calls herself
    a handmaid of the Lord.
Gabriel's first annunciation was about a child being born
    of an old married couple
    who had never been blessed with children.
Gabriel's second annunciation was about a child being born
    to a virgin who had not even chosen her wedding date.
In the first annunciation Gabriel gives the task
    of naming the child John
    to his father, which was the ordinary
    patriarchal way of doing things.
In the second annunciation Gabriel gives the task
    of naming the child Jesus
    not to Joseph but to the mother, Mary.

Looking back on George Will's list
    with the images of Gabriel's
    revolutionary annunciation to Mary in mind,
    you wonder why none of his candidates were women,
    why none were humble,
    why none were poor and powerless,
    why none were mothers.

If there had been a *Time* magazine in the year 1000
    choosing "The Person of the Millennium,"
    I trust that the humble maidservant of Nazareth,
    whose *yes* to God not only ushered in the first millennium
    but a kingdom that would be without end,
    would at least have made most experts' short lists.

Every once in a while Geraldo, Phil and Oprah trot onto stage
    a group of unwed mothers.
They are what Jesse Jackson calls "babies making babies."
What often emerges from the interviews of these girls
    is that in their minds,

motherhood is about possessing.
One's heart aches for these young mothers
  whose own childhood was abusive
  and left them with feelings of loneliness and lack of self-worth.

But Mary teaches all of us,
  mothers, fathers, children, adults, wed and unwed,
  that salvation comes not from clutching to what is "ours"
  but from letting go and sharing what has been given to us,
  even when we seem powerless and small.
"I am the maidservant of the Lord.
Let it be done to me as you say."

Our Advent liturgy ends with
  a woman waiting.
Mary's waiting reminds us that
  waiting in hope for God's gift
  is what makes God's people so unique.
Mary was the first to teach us that Christmas
  is not primarily about getting
  but about giving and letting go
  so that Christ could come to save.
That's why she's so high on the church's list of
  Christians of all time.

6
HOW TO BE AN ADVENT PERSON
Third Sunday of Advent (C)

- Zephaniah 3:14–18
- Philippians 4:4–7
- Luke 3:10–18

When I was a kid, I was confused about the language
  adults sometimes used.
They said that when they went to work they had
  "to punch a clock."
"Why take it out on a poor clock?" I thought.
  "Adults are weird."
I remember too how adults would speak certain words
  in hushed tones.
When the adults of my family
  spoke of certain women, they said,
  "Did you hear? She's expecting."
  "Expecting?
  Expecting what?" I wondered.

In our current TV age,
  kids and adults share a more common language.
Words like "pregnant" are available to us all.
Our new common language has erased
  many of the old expressions like
  "she's expecting."

I thought about that quaint phrase the other day because
  it seems to capture the melody of this lovely season.
Mary is expecting new life in a mysterious, wondrous way.
Elizabeth, her old retired cousin is expecting the same.
Even the men of Advent,

like the prophets Isaiah and Baruch
and today's Zephaniah,
are acting like expectant mothers;
    they feel new life kicking in their weary nation's womb.
And with all his ups and downs,
    Paul is convinced that the Lord is coming back,
    and he's expecting it to happen soon.

Today's central Advent figure is John the Baptist
    whose sermons were dead serious
    and whose God was as tough as nails.
John came from "the old school."
He had enough *chutzpah* to call his congregation
    a "brood of snakes."
John was no wimp in the pulpit.
He baptized the people and told them that
    they had better clean up their act.

John did all this because something in his prophet's gut
    told him that the old times were coming to an end.
John smelled something out there in the desert air;
    he sensed it in the crowds who came out to hear him.
They "were full of anticipation, wondering in their hearts."
John heard the rumblings of violent people who were planning
    a bloody uprising against the Roman army.
John looked around and expected something was coming
    that was going to be totally new.
His expectations kept his popularity from getting to his head.
John was expecting someone mightier than himself.

John the Baptist was right.
Something totally new did appear,
    but not exactly the way John had expected it.
The reign of God burst forth with the coming of Jesus
    who broke the ancient cycle of sin and death
    in a way that startled even John the Baptist.

All of the characters of the great drama of Advent
    are people who are expecting.
The word expect comes from the Latin, *spectare,* which means
    "to look out of."
People who are expecting

are those who are looking out of their present situation
    to something new that is going to occur.

About a year ago, a friend of mine shared her expectancy with me.
She wasn't expecting a child.
She was on her way to becoming a grandmother.
She had sensed that she was trapped,
    that her life held little meaning or joy.
But somehow my friend was expecting
    that something or someone new
    was calling out to her.
Expectancy is not without its terror.
She was both curious and frightened
    about what was around the corner.

Through trial, risk, prayer and professional counseling,
    my friend is now at peace.
She's discovered what it was that she was expecting:
    a new life.
She realizes that for many years she had allowed herself
    to be a co-dependent of her alcoholic husband.
They were trapped in a marriage that was not life-giving,
    that robbed them both of peace and hope.
They have both made the decision to break the cycle of violence
    and choose life.

They are not unlike many people in our day
    who are discovering that the way to happiness and life
    is not a continuance of the same old pattern of despair.
People are discovering that
    the reason they are abusing themselves with alcohol and drugs,
    the reason they are abusing their children and spouses,
    is not because they are bad people
    but because they, too, were victims
    of these addictions as children.
For groups such as Adult Children of Alcoholics,
    the phrase "breaking the cycle" means a decision
    to stop the violence not only for themselves,
    but for their spouses and their children's sake.
There are many people like my friend
    who are expecting a new life.
Many of them are in your lives as well.

They are in your class,
  in your neighborhood,
  in your workplace,
  in your parish community,
  in your family.
They are enslaved in a vicious cycle of violence and despair.
They put up such a good front that you would never know
  what hell they are going through.
But once in a while
  they do break down
  and like the people who came to John the Baptist,
  they ask, "What ought we to do?"

When that happens,
  pay attention to their expectancy.
Know that God is breaking through in their lives.
Encourage them to expect that there is a way out.
Get them help.
In doing so,
  you will be joining that long line of people of God
  throughout the history of salvation
  whose special vocation is to be Advent people—
  to expect the best.
The best is yet to come!

CHRISTMAS

7
CHRISTMAS IS FOR SEEING
Christmas (Mass at Dawn)

- Isaiah 62:11–12
- Titus 3:4–7
- Luke 2:15–20

Among the many crosses I inflicted on my parents as a child
   was my enthusiasm to volunteer for everything.
The teacher would ask, "Who would like to . . . ?"
Before she finished the question,
   I was already waving my hand.
One year, just before Christmas,
   my fifth grade teacher asked
   if someone would volunteer to write
   a little play for the P.T.A. pageant.
Only two kids volunteered, Shirley Savino and I.
Luckily my hand went up first.
Shirley was not amused.
She sulked for days.

My little play was not original.
It was just a kid's rendition of the birth of Christ,
   beginning with the knock on the door of many inns,
   and culminating with most of the fifth grade singing
   the angel's song of "Peace on Earth."
Naturally, I gave myself the part of Joseph.
When I told Shirley about what I had written,
   she challenged my creative genius by crying out:
      "You didn't write that story;
      I saw that before in church!"

I'm not sure whether it was
   my first act of Christian reconciliation
   or a cagey act of preventing her from ruining my play;
   but I decided, then and there,
   to give the part of Mary to Shirley.
At any rate, the play was a stunning success
   with the kids, the P.T.A.,
   and especially Shirley Savino.
Maybe the reason that things went so well was that everyone,
   including a little Joseph draped in his father's bathrobe,
   saw the birth of the Prince of Peace
   in a new way,
   with eyes of faith.

On Christmas eve,
   for about the past twenty years,
   I try to find some quiet time to read
   one of my favorite stories,
   A *Christmas Memory* by Truman Capote.[1]
The story centers around two characters,
   Buddy, who is Truman as a little boy,
   and a "sixty-something" woman,
   whom Buddy simply calls, "my best friend."
They live in an old southern farmhouse
   inhabited by other relatives,
   who are snooty and mean.
The old woman is mentally retarded
   but her childlike schemes
   fire the imagination of the orphan boy.

There is a moving scene in which the relatives
   exchange Christmas gifts.
Buddy is crestfallen when he unwraps his gifts which consist of

---

[1] Truman Capote and Eleanor Perry, "A Christmas Memory," the script, as found in *Triology: An Experiment in Multimedia*, Truman Capote, Eleanor Perry, Frank Perry (New York: Collier Books, 1969) pp. 248–252.

"socks, a Sunday school shirt, some handkerchiefs, a hand-me-down
sweater and a year's subscription to a religious magazine for children:
The Little Shepherd."
The old woman is equally disappointed with her gifts
    of pot holders and a white knitted shawl.
But suddenly, her eyes begin to twinkle mischievously
    as she coaxes Buddy out of the parlor and into the kitchen.
There, under a little Christmas tree,
    that the old woman had somehow managed to concoct
    with simple bits and pieces,
    they open up the gifts they have made for each other.
They give each other the same thing—a kite.
"Oh, Buddy! Mine's just beautiful!"
Buddy stares at his blue kite
    scattered with gold good conduct stars and says,
    "Not as beautiful as mine!"
"Oh how I wanted to give you a bicycle!" she exclaims.
Buddy says, "I wanted to give you a whole pound of
    chocolate covered cherries!"
She laments, "It's bad enough in life to do without something *you*
    want . . . what gets my goat is not being able to give somebody
    something you want *them* to have."

The mood changes when Buddy's friend yells out,
    "The wind is blowing!"
They rush outside to try out their new kites.
"It's a radiant Christmas day. The grass of the pasture is golden against
the dazzling blue of the sky. The Woman looks about them, her eyes
feasting on the wonder of God's work, on Buddy's contented small boy's
face, on the whole lovely world stretching to the horizon."

The woman then says,
    "My, how foolish I am! You know what I've always thought? I've always
    thought a body would have to be sick and dying before they saw the
    Lord. And I imagined that when He came it would be like looking at
    a Baptist window: pretty as colored glass with the sun pouring
    through . . . such a shine you don't know it's getting dark. And it's
    been a comfort to me to think of that shine—taking away all the
    spooky feeling. But I'll wager it never happens. I'll wager at the very
    end a body realizes the Lord has already shown Himself. . . . As for
    me, I could leave the world with today in my eyes."

Our Christmas gospel today is not about
  the flutter of angels and their mighty chorale.
Luke tells us that they've gone back to heaven.
The story is about simple folk,
    shepherds who see with eyes of faith:
    "Let us go over to Bethlehem and see this event
    which the Lord has made known to us."
If we gaze upon Christmas with eyes that are not of the Spirit,
    with eyes that are cynical and not open to awe,
    with a vision that refuses to believe the impossible
    and adore the Gift before us,
    we will never know the joy of the shepherds
    who praised God for all they had heard and seen.

Seeing is believing.
Faith is not a head trip nor a magical mystical sideshow.
Faith is seeing the Gift before us
    with new eyes and new hearts.
Don't be afraid this Christmas
    to see what God has given you.
Don't be afraid to be like the simplé shepherds
    and joyfully tell the world, not "Season's Greetings,"
    but that the Prince of Peace is born again
    to those who are willing
    to open wide their eyes.

8
COMING HOME FOR CHRISTMAS
Christmas (Mass During the Day)

- Isaiah 52:7–10
- Hebrews 1:1–6
- John 1:11–18

Since Thanksgiving time,
    the music of Christmas has filled the air
    of Dart Drug, Safeway and Hechinger's.[1]
I imagine that the people
    who work at the checkout counters of those stores
    are relieved that Christmas is here
    and thus they are free from Christmas elevator music
    for eleven more months.
Have you ever noticed how slow the songs are in Christmas muzak?
They are so slow that you can actually understand the words.
Mostly the words are about
    dreams of simpler and happier times.
They are about dreaming
    of a white Christmas
    and chestnuts roasting on the open fire.
Mostly they are about dreaming
    that we are back home:
    "I'll be home for Christmas, you can count on me . . ."

---

[1] Local stores.

41

But the reason why we're not only merry
   but also a little teary-eyed at Christmas
   is that many of us can never go home again.
We're grown up with houses of our own.
Life isn't simple anymore.
"I'll be home for Christmas,
   but only in my dreams."

Christmas comes and bids us dream and remember
   when we were home for Christmas,
   when we were children
   and all *was* calm and all *was* bright.

Home for me as a child was growing up
   in a Polish-American family in Pennsylvania.
Our parents religiously followed the traditional ritual
   of the Christmas Eve meal, *vigilia.*
The meal would not begin until the first star was spotted.
In those days,
   Christmas Eve was a day of fast and abstinence.
After fasting all day, my brothers and I
   became expert star-gazers.
In the middle of the table loaded with Polish delicacies,
   there was a loaf of bread nestled on a bed of straw.
After my Dad prayed grace,
   he would offer my Mom a piece of the blessed wafer,
   called an *opaltek.*
As they broke bread,
   he asked forgiveness for the rough times he caused her during
   the past year
   and then wished her a merry Christmas.
He did the same to all the kids and relatives at the table.
My Mom offered the same breaking of the bread.
Down the line we all took turns.
Since I was the youngest,
   I was the last to offer the *opaltek.*
I did it as quickly as I could because by then I was starved.

There were many other lovely customs at that Christmas Eve meal
   but the one that intrigued me the most
   was the place that was set for the "unseen guest."

My parents had told us year after year,
   "God came to us on the first Christmas
   but the world did not know who he was . . .
   and his own did not accept him."
We were told that one day Christ would come again
   and this time we should accept him into our home
   as we would an honored guest
   at the most precious meal in the year.

One Christmas Eve
   when I had reached the sophisticated age of ten
   and had begun to wonder about the real meaning of such rituals,
   there was a knock on the door.
Could it be, after all these years,
   the unseen guest my parents had been preaching about?
I was about to be a true believer again
   until I was astonished by the man my Dad welcomed
   into our dining room.
He was an old familiar character.
He was what we called in those days, "an old drunk,"
   who bummed the streets and once in a while
   painted for food and booze.
Nobody ever knew his real name,
   and so we called him "Painter."
Needless to say, after all these years,
   I was disappointed that the unseen guest
   who finally came to dinner was Painter!
Now, I could understand my Mom inviting him to dinner.
She was always a soft-touch for giving Painter sandwiches
   when he knocked on the back door.
But I was shocked by Dad who never seemed to like Painter.
"I'll do my own painting," he would say.
   "We don't need *him!*"
But my Dad not only sat Painter down to dinner,
   he seemed honest-to-God delighted that
   he had knocked at our door.
I remember how Painter's smell of Four Roses and Lucky Strikes
   competed with my Mom's *pierogi.*
My brothers and I gasped
   as Dad broke the blessed wafer with Painter
   and served him like an honored guest.

My parents never spoke the words,
    but from their simple welcoming of the stranger to our home
    that Christmas Eve,
    we never forgot the message.

For centuries, God's people had been dreaming
    of going back home.
Even in the midst of exile,
    prophets like Isaiah were preaching this *good news.*
The people of Israel believed that
    the homecoming God would give his people
    was not some empty promise.
Indeed, the whole mission of Jesus was
    to bring the outcasts, the displaced, and the rejected
    home again.

The feast of Christmas touches our hearts and makes us dream
    because it is a celebration of God's homecoming.
"The Word became flesh and made his dwelling among us."
This is the wild and wonderful meaning of Christmas:
    God abandons heaven and comes into our home:
Our home, where life is never perfect,
    where people are often hurting
    and fearful of returning love,
    where even the most cherished religious rituals become empty
    at times.
But those who believe in God
    know that God comes to us in the most unexpected ways,
    in the most unexpected people.
Those who believe in God know that when they open the door
    to the unseen guest,
    they become "children of God."

LENT

9
THE DESERT *AND* THE MOUNTAIN
Second Sunday of Lent (A)

- Genesis 12:1–4
- 2 Timothy 1:8–10
- Matthew 17:1–9

Who says nobody pays attentions to homilies these days?
Last week, at New York's St. Patrick's Cathedral,
   Cardinal O'Connor's homily for the First Sunday of Lent
   made newspaper headlines and was featured
   in all the major TV news reports.
The New York tabloids had a field day with such headlines as:
   "Cardinal Blasts Satan Songs."
Because last Sunday featured the character of Satan
   tempting Jesus with riches, power and glory,
   the cardinal dared to speak about a subject most preachers
   are embarrassed to mention:
   the influence of Satan on our lives today.
He took on some rock music, whose lyrics are sometimes satanic.
Ozzy Osbourne was not amused.
The cardinal even went so far as to mention in his homily
   that there had been two exorcisms performed
   in the archdiocese of New York last year.
News of exorcisms is usually kept quiet,
   especially by bishops.
And so that juicy bit of news
   titillated the tabloid journalists.

But what will the cardinal preach about this morning?
There are no devils in the gospel story for
   the Second Sunday of Lent,
   only some disciples on a high with their Master.

I'll bet you all the change in your rice bowls
    that the cardinal's homily for this Sunday
    will not make the headlines.
It's beyond our wildest imagination that Monday's New York *Post*
    will splash on its first page the startling news that
    "Cardinal Claims Some People in New York
    Have Seen God This Past Year."

Why is it that we are more fascinated by
    the bad news of Satan
    than the good news of Jesus Christ?
Why is it that we seem more fascinated by signs of evil
    than signs of God's grace?
Maybe the worst temptation of Satan is not to believe
    in the good news of God's presence in our lives.

That is the reason why we have today's story of the transfiguration.
In fact, it's the reason why St. Matthew recorded the story
    for the people of his time:
    to keep sight of God's presence in their lives.
In Matthew's time,
    the people were beginning to wonder
    if the good news of risen life would ever come to them.
They were tempted to believe in the bad news
    instead of the good news
And so Matthew reminded them that
    even when Jesus was about to die,
    even when the disciples were fearful of that death,
    Jesus revealed the good news that God was with them.

Centuries later, the early Christians,
    called the catechumens,
    were also beginning to wonder
    about the good news of God's presence.
In just a few weeks they were about to be baptized
    and they were beginning to get cold feet.
They were tempted to believe not the good news,
    but the bad news
    that they would never be able to break from their bad habits
        of a lifetime
    and begin the new life of a Christian.

And so the church on the Second Sunday of Lent
    gave the catechumens this dazzling story of God's presence;
    like the disciples who lay paralyzed on the ground in fear,
    they heard Jesus tell them:
    "Get up! Do not be afraid.
    Don't stay on the ground.
    Look up.
    Listen to my beloved Son on whom my favor rests.
    Listen to him."

Now I have no doubts about
    the presence of diabolical evil in this world.
Boarder babies,
    the ovens of Auschwitz,
    drunk drivers and oil slicks
    are grim reminders of
    the darker side of the human spirit.
But I also agree with St. Paul that
    "where sin abounds, grace abounds more."
In other words,
    I believe in the real presence of God in our world,
    a presence more powerful and energizing than
    a shelf-load of satanic songs.

Lent is a time for us to affirm our belief in the risen life,
    in the presence of God in our world,
    in the good news that Christ has overcome evil and sin,
    not only the diabolical evil that makes the news,
    but the petty evil that lurks in our hearts.
Lent is that special time for us to believe more
    in the power of the good news
    than in the sadness of the bad news.

The scriptures that we hear during Lent feature
    two geographical spots:
    the desert and the mountain.
Last week we were in the desert;
    today we're on top of the mountain.
We need to stand in both spots during Lent,
    the desert *and* the mountain.

In the desert, we encounter the devil,
   we face our guilt and the evil that abounds in our world.
The Christian life is impossible without the desert.

But it is also impossible without the mountain top
   where we can breathe fresh air and see everything
   in a new light.
It is good for us to be on the mountain,
   where we can see and listen to God in a new way.

This Lent we must find a way to go to two places:
   to some desert where we can face our devil
   and to some mountain top where we can hear the good news
   that our God is greater than any evil we can ever imagine.

10
THIRST THAT LEADS TO LIFE
Third Sunday of Lent (A)

- Exodus 17:3–7
- Romans 5:1–2,5–8
- John 4:5–42

Two weeks ago, during spring break,
    I enjoyed a visit with
    my brother and his wife and family
    in my hometown of Scranton, Pennsylvania.
At dinnertime one night,
    my sister-in-law Joannie complained
    about the water in Scranton.
Joannie is one of those precious few left in the world who has
    few complaints.
Therefore, when she complained about the water,
    I listened.
It seems the many years of reckless strip mining
    have left the region with water
    that not only tastes foul
    but poses serious health problems.
Now my family has to cart gallon jugs of mineral water
    from the supermarket each week.
The situation is so bad
    that it has turned even cheerful Joannie
    into a grumbling environmentalist.
When people thirst, they change behavior.

The story we just heard about Moses and the people in the desert
    is from chapters 14–17 of Exodus
    which is sometimes referred to as
    the "Book of Grumblings."

The people grumbled because they too were having a water crisis.
The desert sun had not only tested their thirst
    but also their faith in God's plan.
They wondered,
    "Is the Lord in our midst or not?"
A lack of water
    turned these once committed believers in the exodus
    into grumbling skeptics.
When people thirst, they change behavior.

Even Jesus seems to change in John's gospel
    because he is thirsty.
John stresses Jesus' divinity
    more than any of the other gospel writers.
But in the story of Jesus and the Samaritan woman,
    John gives us a poignant glimpse of Jesus
    in the fullness of his humanity.
Sweaty and exhausted from a long journey,
    Jesus sits down by the well
    at noon when the heat is at its peak.
So what that the person with the water jar is a woman
    and a Samaritan as well?
So what that there are strict rules
    against Jews talking with such kind?
Jesus is thirsty.
He looks at her and says,
    "Give me a drink."

What we might miss in this story is that
    the woman also is thirsty.
She has carted her jar more than half a mile
    from her home in Sychar.
Some have wondered why she came to this well
    since there was a well in Sychar.
Could it be that she was also a public sinner who was forbidden
    to draw water in her home town?
Whatever the reason, like Jesus, the Samaritan woman
    was also thirsty
    and anxious to get back home
    with her jar filled to the brim.

But the two thirsty and weary strangers
    have a remarkable conversation—
    so remarkable that John notes that the woman
    left her water jar at the well.
That jar, which was once one of her most valued treasures,
    is now just a memory.
She drank from the Living Water
    and now has a new thirst;
    she is a new woman
    with a new mission.

In state senates across our nation
    there is a lot of grumbling going on about
    the most explosive and divisive issue in American politics:
    abortion.
Many anti-abortion leaders believe that the reason
    why abortion is such an uncomfortable issue for politicians
    is that it deals with many
    conflicting and fundamental issues
    like life, privacy and religion.
The abortion issue presents a stinging dilemma
    especially for Catholic politicians.
They are aware of our church's teaching on the sacredness of life
    from conception to the grave.
They are painfully aware of the destruction of human life in our nation
    where over four thousand abortions
    take place each day.
Catholic politicians are also civil servants who must legislate
    in a democracy which is
    a patchquilt of ideas and convictions.

Our former Surgeon General, Dr. C. Everett Koop, has stated that
    the abortion issue threatens
    the very future of our nation as a democracy.
Koop says that no single issue can divide this nation in two
    as abortion can.
He has likened it to the issue of slavery
    which ripped our country apart
    and brought about the Civil War.
If you listen to the grumbling of both sides,
    pro-life and pro-choice,

you will hear the rumblings of war.
Both sides talk about "winning the battle" and use other such
   bellicose phrases.
In the name of life,
   both sides often destroy
   even the possibility of human dialogue.
Molly Yard fires off her salvos at pro-life leaders
   with the stubbornness of Rambo.
In the heat of the battle,
   some anti-abortion religious leaders
   often forget the compassion of Jesus.

If just a portion of the energies,
   the lobby money,
   the brains of both sides
   could be set aside for a life-giving conversation,
   maybe a miracle might happen.

The gospel today is startling because it shows what can happen
   when weary strangers meet
   and have a life-giving conversation.
The miracle at the well began with a simple request from a thirsty man,
   "Give me a drink."
The abortion issue will not be solved by hardened hearts,
   but with hearts like that of Jesus at the well.
As Catholic Christians we must drop our war-like stance
   and learn how to talk to pro-choice leaders
   without violating our commitment to the sacredness of life.
In other words, we must begin
   to talk and act like Jesus.

11
THE PASCHAL MYSTERY:
SNOW ON THE LILACS
Passion (Palm) Sunday (A)

- Matthew 21:1-11

(*The Sacramentary* states that "a brief homily may be given" after the gospel. It also states that "a brief homily may be given" after the reading of the passion. I prefer the first option. If the passion is proclaimed in good dramatic fashion, it seems superfluous to preach even "a brief homily" afterward. The character of the homily following the gospel should be an invitation for the congregation to enter into the paschal mystery of Holy Week.)

Up the road from where I live stands Mia's Nursery.
Mia is a tiny Korean woman who has two giant green thumbs.
Her flowers and vegetable plants are the biggest and the best
   in Prince William County.
But April this year has been the cruelest month for Mia.
Each sundown she has to cover her pansies and geraniums
   because of the freaky winter weather that has come our way.
It's not supposed to snow in April.
The delicate azaleas and lovely lilacs don't deserve
   this painful shock.

Palm Sunday is a lot like
   the snow on our lilacs.
We celebrate today not some neat lesson
   nor a clear-cut article of faith
   but a paradox,
   a mystery,
   a mingling of forces

both good and evil,
both glorious and cruel.
We begin with a brassy march into Jerusalem
with palms in our hands and praise on our lips:
"Blessed is he who comes in the name of the Lord!"
But in a few minutes there will be a chill in the air
when we will cry out,
"Crucify him! Crucify him!"

Like the snow on our lilacs,
it's all so mysterious.
That is what this day
and the holy week that follows are all about:
mystery.
We began our liturgy by proclaiming that
"for five weeks of Lent we have been preparing,
by works of charity and self-sacrifice,
for the celebration of our Lord's paschal mystery."

"Paschal mystery" means the celebration
of the death *and* the resurrection of our Lord.
What makes it a mystery is that it is a mingling of both.
We cannot separate one from the other.
Jesus embraced both
the palms and the passion.
He rode triumphantly as king into the city of Jerusalem,
convinced not just of the blessings of the crowd
but of the blessing of his Father.
But his life was also filled with passion,
with the pain and absurdity of life.
He didn't ignore the reality of sin and despair;
he cried out in anguish:
"My God, my God, why have you forsaken me?"

We Christians always mess things up when we try
to collapse the mystery—
when we deny either the reality of sin and death
or the blessing of God's promise of new life.
This Sunday is called by two names,
Passion Sunday and Palm Sunday.

It's a reminder that life does have two sides,
    a reminder of the mystery of life that Jesus embraced.

Coming home from church one snowy afternoon,
    Emerson wrote:
    "The snow was real but the preacher, spectral."
In other words, the preaching that Emerson heard that day
    made no impact
    because it failed to recognize
    the cold and absurd side of life.
It was a denial of the reality of sin and death.

It's easy to deny the snow on the lilacs.
Sin and death are denied in our times with great artistry.
Life is cheap and so we don't bat an eye when
    limbs are ripped off and blood splatters
    our TV and movie screens.
Somehow the hungry faces of children from the third world,
    the oil-drenched birds in Alaska,
    the wild images of the homeless
    can all be denied by our remote controls.
We're manipulated to believe that we are supermen and superwomen
    who with the right amount of bucks or drugs or looks
    can breeze through life without a bump.

It's also quite easy these days to deny
    the promise of the lilacs,
    to come to the conclusion that it's all hopeless,
    that there is no rhyme nor reason to what God sends our way.
We are tempted to live out of terror
    rather than in a trust
    in our God who is with us and for us.
It has become easier to ride out of the city than into it,
    to break our promises rather than to keep them,
    to deny the possibility of a new beginning.

But this morning we ride with confidence
    into the city with Jesus
    and we also cry out with him from the cross.
On Friday we will dare to call the day "good,"
    because even in the midst of death,

we will proclaim life.
And on Easter Sunday, in the midst of new life,
   our risen Lord will greet us with still pierced hands.
His mystery is our mystery!
His death, our death!
His victory, our victory!

12
DO WE NEED LENT NOW?
First Sunday of Lent (C)

- Deuteronomy 26:4–10
- Romans 10:8–13
- Luke 4:1–13

February 12 is the earliest possible day for
  the First Sunday of Lent.
We've just about packed away
  our Christmas ornaments and unused presents
  when we're invited to the church's season of spring
  for renewal and reflection.
But it feels too cold for Lent.
We'd rather snuggle up as couch potatoes than
  prepare our rice bowls.
Do we need Lent now?

There was a time, of course,
  when all Christians thought
  they didn't need Lent.
After all, they had been baptized in the Lord;
  they were filled with the Holy Spirit
  and lived life quite differently from the pagans.
The first real Lenten people were not Christians,
  but those preparing to become Christians.
They wore sackcloth and ashes
  and lived the days before Easter
  as repentant sinners.
But all of that changed
  when the old-timers in the Christian community
  noticed something remarkable at the Easter baptism.
They were struck by the joy and the radiant faces

of those just baptized.
They too longed to experience the thrill of new birth,
    new strength, new life.
They realized that they had become too ho-hum in their faith
    and decided to do something about it.

And so, the next year, some Christians began to join the catechumens
    in their preparation for baptism at Easter.
They too took on sackcloth and ashes
    and lived the days before Easter as repentant sinners.
They did this so that they could feel once again
    the joy of rebirth at Easter.
And that's how Lent gradually came to the church,
    out of a need.

The liturgy for this First Sunday of Lent
    focuses on a need that Jesus had before he began to save the world.
Even though he had just been baptized
    and was "full of the Holy Spirit,"
    he felt a need to go into the desert.

In the desert Jesus realized who he was
    and what he was called to do.
In the desert Jesus found his first temptations.
He was not the first to be tempted there.
His ancestors faced the same tests.
In its desert wanderings,
    Israel too was worried about food and safety.
Israel too was tempted
    to bow down to the golden calf
    rather than to the one true God.

But in the desert, Jesus learned that God cannot be bought
    and that life is more than bread
    or fleeting moments of magic and glory.
Right after Jesus left the desert,
    he went back to his hometown of Nazareth.
There in the synagogue,
    he proclaimed a passage from Isaiah,
    but he spoke Isaiah's words as his own:
        "The Spirit of the Lord is upon me,
        because I am anointed to bring glad tidings to the poor.

The Spirit of the Lord has sent me
to proclaim liberty to the captives
and recovery of sight to the blind,
to let the oppressed go free,
and to proclaim a year acceptable to the Lord" (Luke 4:18).

After the desert,
    after his first temptation,
    after his first Lent,
    Jesus realized who he was and what he was called to do.

One Ash Wednesday, many years ago,
    while I was wondering how to face another Lent,
    I received a phone call from a former student.
He had left the seminary
    and was now a struggling graduate student.
The young man was crying out for help.
When I got to his apartment,
    I found a tortured soul,
    filled with self-doubt and booze.

Eventually, I got him to go to his first AA meeting.
But even though he was an alcoholic,
    he told me that he couldn't go back to another AA meeting
    because "I'm not like those people."

I've never forgotten that line,
    "I'm not like those people."
It taught me that the first temptation to avoid choosing life
    is to convince yourself
    that somehow you are different,
    that you don't share the pain of life,
    that you don't need to go into the desert.

The early Christians, even though they were baptized
    and convinced of their importance,
    learned from the desert experience of Lent that
    they too were in need of renewal
    and of finding out who they were
    and who God was calling them to be.
Jesus, just baptized by John and "full of the Holy Spirit,"
    went into the desert

and came out with a gospel
and a firm faith in his Father
that he would take to Calvary.

My young friend was wrong.
We are like *those* people
   who share a common struggle and a common pain.
We are all driven by the same doubts.
We sometimes make choices about
   the most important events of our lives
   without reflection,
   without faith,
   without prayer,
   without God.
We cannot force Lent upon ourselves.
Each of us must find a need for it—
   a need to go into the desert
   to face both our gifts and our limits,
   a need to face ourselves,
   our demons,
   and our God.

Even though Lent is early
   and it all seems risky,
   let's go into the desert together!

13
TRACING OR ERASING IN THE SAND?
Fifth Sunday of Lent (C)

- Isaiah 43:16–21
- Philippians 3:8–14
- John 8:1–11

From the beginning,
    folks have been more than curious about what
    Jesus traced on the sand.
St. Jerome was one of the first serious speculators.
He guessed that when Jesus bent down,
    he traced the sins of those men
    seeking to stone the woman to death.
Some scholars have suggested that Jesus' tracing on the sand
    was a gesture of silence;
    he was like Isaiah's "suffering servant,"
    who "opened not his mouth" to those seeking to trap him.
Some have suggested a spiritual reason—
    Jesus' tracing was a silent time to pray
    to the Father for advice.
Others have offered more practical reasons—
    Jesus was simply doodling in the sand
    until the time was right to speak
    or even waiting for the woman's lover
    to be dragged before the crowd of accusers
    since strict observance of the Mosaic law
    required both adulterers be stoned to death,
    both the man *and* the woman.
I would like to add yet another theory
    to this curious gesture of Jesus.
Maybe Jesus wasn't tracing but erasing on the sand.

That theory makes sense when we hear this gospel
    in light of our first reading from the prophet Isaiah.

The reading from Isaiah comes from a time
   when Israel was held captive in Babylon,
   when the only hope left was the memory of a glorious past.
And so while Israel sweated it out
   in a foreign land for fifty years,
   the only consolation left for the people was to sing about
   the wonderful exodus time
   when God first freed Israel from Egypt.
In other words,
   the only consolation left for the people in Babylon
   was for them to remember the "good old days"
   when God was on *their* side.

But what is so jolting about this reading from Isaiah
   is that God tells the people to "cut it out."
   "Remember not the events of the past,
   the things of long ago consider not;
   see, I am doing something new!"
God tells the people to take a big eraser and wipe out the past,
   and not just the bad and sinful memories,
   but the good memories as well.
As long as the people dwelt on the past,
   including their past glories,
   they could never make a fresh interpretation of the present
   and believe in a God who would lead them out of Babylon
   and bring them back to the promised land.

And so when Jesus bent down,
   he may have been erasing in the sand
   not just the sins of the men and the woman in their midst,
   but all their past glories as well.
Jesus may have been erasing
   all those patriarchal interpretations
   of religious and social law
   that kept women "in their place."
Jesus bends down and erases in the sand
   not just their sins
   but the narrow interpretations they still clung to.

Yesterday in Rome
   a four-day meeting ended between
   thirty-four American archbishops

and Vatican officials.
The meeting was designed to help both Rome and the U.S. church
    to understand one another.

One of the hottest moments of the meeting in Rome came on Friday
    when the church leaders addressed the serious problems of
    sexual promiscuity
    and the alarming statistics of abortion and divorce
    in the United States.
Fingers were pointed at the American church
    for granting too many annulments.
Some Vatican officials blamed the ease of getting annulments
    on women religious employed now
    in diocesan marriage tribunals.
One cardinal declared,
    "Women religious can be very helpful in dealing with marriage cases,
    but we have to be careful that their tender hearts do not play tricks
    on them."

Today, in Rome, those men heard at mass
    this same gospel of compassion.
We can only pray that they, too, paid attention to Jesus
    erasing in the sand
    not just the sins of the doctors of the law and the Pharisees
    but the tired old memories and interpretations
    some still clung to.

What the church needs at this present moment
    is not to cling to the male domination of the past,
    but to pay attention to
    the tender and tough hearts of women,
    so long ignored.
What the church needs now
    is not to cling to the good old days of power
    when the church spoke and people jumped,
    but to listen to the struggles and the joys
    of ordinary people today,
    and then speak against sin with Jesus' voice of compassion.

It is something of an irony that we have
    this gospel of compassion
    at the conclusion of the meeting in Rome.

This particular gospel story didn't appear
  in the original manuscripts of John.
It wasn't inserted into John's gospel
  until the third or fourth century.
It seems that the reason this story took so long
  to be included in the canon of the Bible
  is that during that period,
  church authorities were trying to enforce
  a strict discipline over marriages.
The story of the woman caught in adultery seemed at that time
  to encourage laxity in marriage standards.
Of course, this was a false impression.
After all, Jesus did say to the woman,
  "From now on, avoid this sin."
Jesus named sin *as* sin.
But he also looked at the woman and the men
  in their present moment and announced
  the forgiveness of God.

Thank God some of our American bishops had the good sense
  to speak up at the meeting in Rome.
They said,
  "Before you judge us and throw your stones at us,
  come to the United States and see for yourselves what a church
    we have."
Thank God some of our American bishops have the courage
  to read the signs of the times
  and address such serious issues as sexism in our world
  and in our church.
In their working document,
  Partners in the Mystery of Redemption,
  they remind us of the equal dignity owed to women.
They quote Pope John Paul II who said,
  "The church proclaims the dignity of women as women . . .
  a dignity equal to men's dignity."
Thank God we have a Savior who bends down and erases in the
    sand
  not only our sins
  but the hindering memories and interpretations
  that still weigh us down.
Thank God this gospel survived the misgivings of religious men.
That's why we can call it "good news!"

EASTER

14
LEAVING THE TOMB
Easter

- Acts 10:34,37–43
- 1 Corinthians 5:6–8
- Mark 16:1–8

There's something about the passion and death of Jesus
    that is still appealing to many people in our time.
Despite the rocky political turmoil in Jerusalem,
    on this Good Friday,
        under the watchful eyes of border policemen,
        pilgrims carried their crosses along the Via Dolorosa.
In the Philippines,
    despite the disapproval
    of the Catholic bishops,
    a crowd of 20,000 watched six people nailed to crosses.
In some countries, pilgrims marched to the cross
    while beating themselves with whips.
In our own area, this past Holy Week, folks flocked
    to a Baptist drive-in passion play in Salisbury, MD.
And in Washington, DC, this Friday,
    Catholic pilgrims carrying crosses down Connecticut Avenue
    during rush hour
    were booed and insulted by passing motorists.

Now these pilgrims were celebrating
    an ancient Christian tradition,
    the adoration of the cross.
That tradition is found at the heart of Good Friday's liturgy:
    "This is the wood of the cross,
    on which hung the Savior of the world.
    Come, let us worship!"

But I sometimes wonder why we seem more passionate and graphic
   in our observance of the passion and death of Jesus
   than of his resurrection.
Why is it that in today's Easter newspaper and television clips
   the images we will see will not be of people celebrating
   the resurrection of Jesus,
   but Easter egg rolls and new spring fashions?

Is it the media's fault?
Some critics have observed
   that every one of this year's Oscar nominations for
     best picture of the year,
   except the winner, *Dances With Wolves,*
   had an unnatural fascination with death.
Is it because violence, war, and destruction
   so flood our society
   that TV producers and newspaper reporters are more eager
   to communicate celebrations of death rather than of life?

Or is it the churches' fault?
Is it because today's preachers are more vocal
   about sin and death
   than about the proclamation of new life
   and the good news of the risen Lord?

Whatever the reason, the church's liturgy
   offers us a more balanced and life-giving response.
The image of the risen Lord in our Easter liturgies
   doesn't deny the passion and death of Jesus.
Peter preaches boldly of how
   "they killed him . . . hanging him on a tree."
Paul proclaims: "Christ our Passover has been sacrificed."
And the risen Lord still bears his wounds.
But they are victory wounds,
   scars from a battle won
   by the Savior.

The people in the Easter stories are much like many of us today.
At first they are more willing to celebrate death than life,
   more overcome by cynicism than faith,
   more concerned about the rituals of death

than the possibilities offered to us by the living God
who raised Jesus from the dead.

Mary Magdalene, Mary the mother of James, and Salome
come to the tomb of Jesus draped in black,
prepared to see a corpse.
Instead, they find the stone rolled back and see an angel
who smells sweeter than all their perfumed oils.
The angel is God's messenger—
not an angel of death but an angel of life.

They come to the tomb looking for Jesus of Nazareth
and leave with the story
of the risen Lord for all the world.
They come in their traditional role of anointing women
and leave the tomb in the radical role
of apostles to the apostles.
They come to the tomb slowly, cautiously,
filled with troublesome thoughts,
like, "Who will roll back the stone for us?"
They leave the tomb running, casting all caution to the wind,
proclaiming the good news that
Jesus has been raised from the dead.

All of the resurrection stories are like this.
They are stories of believers
who at first want to cling to the empty tomb,
to the old yeast which never rises.
But in all the biblical stories of this Easter season,
God tells us not to stay at the tomb
with an old dreary way of looking at life
with sighs and fears.

Jesus is not among the dead.
Jesus does not belong to the past.
The Easter angel tells the women
not to cry at the tomb because Jesus isn't there.
He is in Galilee.
In other words, Jesus invites his followers to find him
in the world, in our families,
in our neighborhoods, in every place where people gather,
for the risen Lord is there.

The message of our Easter liturgy
  is radically different from the message of our times.
It challenges us not to a morbid fascination
  with death and violence,
    but to live the kind of life that Jesus won for us.

It is the Easter life
  where life is always chosen over death;
  where sin is forgiven and forgotten;
  where the making of peace is always more important
  than the making of war;
  where new beginnings are possible
  despite our addictions and our past.

We are believers who venerate,
  even wear, the cross of Jesus.
We are also called to venerate,
  even wear, the risen life of the Christ.

15
HEDGERS AND HUGGERS
Easter

- Acts 10:34,37–43
- Colossians 3:1–4
- John 20:1–9

The month of March is a month of mixture:
    crocuses and snowflakes,
    new buds and dry leaves.
In March the crosswinds blow,
    both cold and warm.
In March we're both heartened by the coming of spring
    and disheartened by that trek to H & R Block.
March is that in-between month when we're not quite sure,
    when we're caught in the middle.
Do I take in the snow shovels or bring out the deck furniture?
March is like our lives,
    a mixture of both sorrow and hope.
And like our lives,
    March tempts us to hedge our bets
    but also invites us to stretch our faith.

Last week Barbara Bush made a visit to some of her neighbors.
It was a visit designed to show the First Lady
    not as one who hedges,
    but as one who goes all the way in love and service.

Mrs. Bush visited Grandma's House on DC's Logan Circle.
It's a home which houses and supports babies and young children
    infected with the HIV virus,
    innocent victims of drug-addicted parents.
Mrs. Bush seemed perfectly at home at Grandma's House.

She played toss ball with the kids and hugged them all.
The administrators of Grandma's House were delighted with the hugs.
They knew that photos of these simple gestures by
    the First Grandma of the Nation
    would do more to dispel prejudice and ignorance
    about working with people with AIDS
    than all the lectures in the world.

But before Mrs. Bush left Grandma's House,
    a thirty-nine year old man with AIDS approached her.
He was the head of Damien Ministries,
    a Catholic group that ministers to people with AIDS.
He thanked her for her hugs of the children
    but pointed out that if she just hugged little kids,
    people might get the wrong message.
He told the First Lady
    that not just innocent little babies with AIDS need hugs,
    but adults as well.
Without a blink of the eye
    Barbara Bush hugged the man warmly
    while the cameras flashed.
The First Lady didn't hedge;
    she went all the way in her demonstration
    of love and service.

The stories of the first Easter people are stories
    of people who at first were hedgers.
We see Mary Magdalene,
    so tough standing at the foot of the cross
    but so hesitant as she sits outside of the empty tomb and cries,
    "The Lord has been taken from the tomb!
    We don't know where they have put him!"
We see Peter the rock who once told Jesus,
    "I'll lay down my life for you."
But now he sits in the high priest's courtyard
    just a few feet away from his Master's torture.
He's a man caught in the middle
    and when put to the test, he hedges.
    "I know not the man."

Even in today's Easter gospel
    we note the hesitancy of the beloved John.
Even though he beat Peter in the race to the tomb,

once he got there,
John hedged.
"He did not enter but bent down to peer in."

The Easter story is not just about the resurrection of the Lord from
    the dead.
It's also the story about the people around the Lord
    who were raised to new life.
It's about all those people who went from being
    hedgers to *huggers.*
In Matthew's gospel,
    even after the women heard the angel tell them,
    "He has been raised, exactly as he promised,"
    we read,
    "They hurried away from the tomb,
    half-overjoyed,
    half-fearful."

At first the disciples of Jesus seemed to "half-believe."
But after they picked up the wrappings lying on the ground,
    after they put their perfumed burial oils back on the shelf,
    they gradually began to realize
    what Jesus had been telling them all along:
    that he was the presence of God who came to bring life
    to those who thought that life was a hopeless task.

The disciples looked back and remembered
    how Jesus had spent so much time and energy
    with those considered hopeless and dead:
    the lepers, those possessed by demons,
    the poor, the widow's son,
    his dead friend Lazarus.
    Jesus sought them out,
    no matter where they were—
    Zacchaeus in the tree,
    Bartimaeus on the side of the road,
    the crazy man from Gerasene whose neighbors had consigned him
    to live in the tombs.
To all the powerless who society had decided might as well be dead,
    Jesus brought life.
Jesus never hedged;
    he hugged them with the power of God and brought them home.

The first Easter people were not so much concerned
　with the mechanics of Jesus coming out of the tomb.
What they really were concerned about was the good news—
　that we who are baptized in Jesus
　are called to live like him.
We are called to believe in the power and the presence of God
　despite the hedging that still goes on in our lives
　and in our world.
We are called to choose life even when we smell death,
　to believe not in spite but in forgiveness,
　to reject the prince of darkness
　and all those agents of death
　who refuse to believe in the possibility of new life.
We are called to hug the powerless and welcome back to life
　those who were lost.

Even though it's March,
　even though we're tempted to hedge,
　even though our lives are full of ambiguity,
　let's rise with Jesus to new life and choose as our song
　a brand new *Alleluia!*

16
WE'RE NOT THERE YET!
Third Sunday of Easter (A)

- Acts 2:14,22–28
- 1 Peter 1:17–21
- Luke 24:13–35

We began our liturgy this morning by singing:
  "Come and Journey with Me."
In recent years, "journey" has become a popular word
  in our hymns and in our homilies
  to describe as best we can
  our Christian lives.
The word "journey" helps to remind us that
  "we're not there yet."
It keeps us from getting puffed up with smugness
  because we believe that we possess the truth.
We're only pilgrims on the way
  who live with a hope that one day we'll arrive.

But there is a journey that many of us make each day
  which leads us to wonder
  if we really ever will make it home.
It's the journey we make each day on I-95 or Route 1.
It causes distress not only to those on the road,
  but to those waiting at home.
Local psychologists are calling that journey
  one of the major stress factors in family conflicts.

Our rush hour traffic happens at about the same time
  that the two disciples made their way home to Emmaus:
  the time when it is "nearly evening,"
  when the "day is practically over."

We'd like to make it home in time to enjoy the kids,
   share stories with the family,
   poke around in the garden,
   sip a drink before dinner.

But just when we're relishing the thought
   of ending our day in peace,
   there comes a stumbling block:
   a tractor trailer overturns;
   there's a sudden rain or snowfall.
These are the pains on our journey
   that make *The War of the Roses*[1] seem like tiddleywinks.

Perhaps the most maddening stumbling block on our way back home
   occurs on gorgeous days like these
   when the sun is so strong
   that we can hardly see where we are going.
Again, we have something in common
   with the two disciples in today's story.
Their journey also was toward a sunset.
Emmaus was a small army town seven miles west of Jerusalem.
When Cleopas and his friend made their journey,
   the sun was sinking.
Some authors have even suggested
   that the reason they didn't recognize the Lord speaking to them
   was because they were so blinded by the light.

Cleopas and his friend represent
   all of us disciples who are blinded
   by our own reasoning.
They represent those of us who think we know
   how the day will end,
   how our lives will end,
   how our world will end.
Their gloom and lost hope comes from the fact that
   they have forgotten
   that they are pilgrims.
They think the journey is over while it has only just begun.

---

[1] A popular film at that time.

They journey into the sunset
   instead of into the rising of the sun.

Last Tuesday there was a front page article
   in the Washington *Post,* entitled:
   "One Couple's Calm Journey into Death."
It was the story of Justin and Betty Bruce Bowersock,
   an eighty-two year old Middleburg, Virginia couple, who,
   according to their daughter,
   decided to "call it a day."
Late Monday afternoon,
   when the sun was setting in Middleburg,
   Justin and Betty had a bitter happy hour.
They sipped their last martinis with an overdose of pills.

What I found strange about the story is how it was reported:
   not as a final story of anguish or defeat.
It was written in heroic terms
   as if suicide were a noble act
   of the acceptance of the end of life.

It is not for us to judge the Bowersocks.
Only God knows what beats in the hearts of women and men
   when they face a horrible turn on their journey.
Even the Bible is careful about judging suicide.
There are two famous suicides in the Bible:
   King Saul falls on his sword and Judas hangs himself.
These two biblical stories are told as stories of sadness.
They are sad stories because they are about holy people
   who forgot that they were pilgrims,
   who were blinded by their own reasoning,
   who thought that they knew the end of the story.

The reason why Catholic teaching rejects
   suicide, euthanasia, abortion and capital punishment
   is that they are acts of sadness.
They are violent acts of hopelessness
   that attempt to end the story
   rather than to wait in hope for God's surprising ending.

Cleopas and his friend took an about-face
   and went back to Jerusalem
   once they recognized the Lord in their lives,

once they recognized the fact that their journey
was not a solo ride—
that the Lord was walking with them,
once they recognized that their journey wasn't over,
but had only just begun.

One of the reasons we celebrate the eucharist each week
is to remind ourselves that we don't know
how our journeys will end.
This lovely story of Emmaus has been likened to our eucharist.
We come to liturgy with our own dashed hopes.
We open up our hearts honestly to the Lord
as pilgrims on the way.
We listen in the liturgy of the word
not for some ancient scripture tale to be explained,
but for some clue as to how our own story is hidden
in God's living word.

Finally we come to the table of the Lord
where Jesus is both guest and host,
where we recognize his presence not only at mass,
but in all our journeys,
even the bewildering ones.
When we learn to celebrate the eucharist like that
then our hearts too will burn.

17
WHY HAVE ALL THE STARS GONE?
Seventh Sunday of Easter (A)

- Acts 1:12–14
- 1 Peter 4:13–16
- John 17:1–11

Ever since Shakespeare's Mark Antony stood up to say,
    "Friends, Romans, countrymen . . ."
    eulogies have been the trickiest of all speeches.
He began by saying that he had "come to bury Caesar,
    not to praise him."
But by the time he ended his eulogy
    he had convinced the crowd that Caesar was not only a ruler
    but a god.

I've noticed similar eulogies in recent months
    written by journalists
    who have mourned the passing of some of our Hollywood stars.
They tell us that Garbo was the most beautiful,
    the most enchanting actress ever to grace the silver screen.
They convince us that Lucille Ball was
    the funniest clown ever on TV.
They praise Jim Henson as
    the most creative puppeteer that ever lived.
They canonize Sammy Davis, Jr. as
    the "world's greatest entertainer."
Always the superlative.
Always the most, the greatest, the best.
These modern-day Mark Antonys try to convince us that
    we will never gaze upon such stars again.
There is something terribly depressing in this kind of talk.
What seems missing is a loss of hope in the future.

I sometimes hear that kind of "lost hope" talk
    from priests who mourn the passing of the kind of church
    they once knew and loved and served.
They realize that our seminaries and convents
    are becoming like those old dilapidated motels we spot along Route 1,
    where the neon sign forever blinks:
    Vacancy.
When I began teaching in the seminary in 1968
    there were more than forty-five thousand seminarians.
This year the number will have dropped
    to less than ten thousand.

Priests say that their greatest fear
    is wondering who will follow after them
    in leading God's people in word and worship.
Because of the decline in the priesthood,
    some bishops have appointed women religious
    as pastoral coordinators of parishes.
Maybe these are the bishops who noticed
    the line in today's reading from Acts:
    "There were some women in their company. . . ."

Other bishops have closed once vibrant parishes
    because they simply did not have the priests to staff them.
When the bishops make these unpleasant decisions
    there are storms of protest from people
    who picket the chancery office.
They remember the good old days when their parish
    was the biggest and the best in the diocese.
How could the bishop be so cruel as to close St. Bridget's?
In a recent study of the lay people
    in the archdiocese of Seattle,
    they listed their greatest fear about the "new" church:
    how they will be able to pass on our Catholic tradition
    to their children.

But not everyone is pessimistic about the church's future.
Once in a while someone will stand up and dare
    to speak words that are both realistic and hopeful.
They are like the poets who end their eulogies by telling us that
    "The best is yet to be."

I heard such a speech last week while I made a retreat
   with my community.
It was delivered at the end of mass on Thursday,
   by Father Fritz Hetzler, a fellow Sulpician,
   who is celebrating his fifty-fifth anniversary of priesthood this year.
As usual, he rambled and talked too long—
   one of the privileges of older people.
He didn't flinch to talk about
   the pain and problems of today's church.
Fritz admitted to us that he's glad he's retired
   and doesn't have to come up with solutions.
But missing in his talk was any sign of triumphalism of the past.
He didn't tell us that the heroes and the heroines were all gone.
Somehow he was able to convey to his beleaguered listeners
   a sense of hope in the future.
He didn't tell us to just "hang in there,"
   but he told us to believe
   in the wonders of God's Spirit who makes all things new.

Because I had the blessed privilege of a week's retreat,
   I had more quality time these last few days
   to reflect on the gospel we heard today.
What struck me most about this prayer of Jesus before his death
   was not just his trust in his Father,
   but also his trust in his disciples.
Jesus doesn't dwell on past glories.
He looks at those who pray with him:
   a weak and motley little group.
But Jesus believes that these eleven
   really do belong to the Father,
   and that through these "earthen vessels"
   his work will carry on.
Jesus prays for his disciples because he believes
   "the best is yet to be."

This prayer of Jesus from the Bible is like the Bible itself.
It is never a closed book of past events
   but a book that is open toward the future;
   it is a book about God's promises.
Today's reading from Acts is the last time
   we will hear of the historical Mary in the Bible.
This last portrait that Luke paints of Mary

is like the first portrait
he painted of her in his gospel.
She is the disciple who is praying and expecting
that great things are going to happen.
That is why we call her the "Mother of the Church."

The God of the Bible never tells us that all the stars have gone,
but bids us pray for those who have yet to shine.
Our God is something like those TV announcements
constantly telling us to
"stay tuned, there is more to follow."
Let us pray this eucharist in the spirit of the prayer of Jesus:
with faith not only in our God
but in those whom God will send us.

18
WHY WE'RE NOT GHOST-BUSTERS
Third Sunday of Easter (B)

- Acts 3:13–15,17–19
- 1 John 2:1–5
- Luke 24:35–48

We miss the obvious,
    what's under our nose.
We walk and talk with *someone* on the road.
We're so wound up with what's happening to us
    that we never realize that something far more important
    has happened to the person next to us.
We talk about our broken hearts
    but we fail to see the stranger's pierced heart.
We're so wrapped up in talking about our own *bad news*
    that we fail to hear our companion's *good news*.

That's what happened to the two disciples on the road to Emmaus.
It was only in the breaking of the bread
    that everything began to make sense.
Despite the rugged cross,
    the nails in his hands and feet,
    the musty tomb,
    despite the stranger's homily (which was biblically based),
    it was only when they noticed how he broke the bread
    that they recognized the risen Lord.
When they saw him doing what he had always done:
    take an ordinary piece of bread,
    break it, give thanks and then pass it around,
    they knew why their hearts were burning back there on the road
    when he spoke with them
    about all that had happened.

The story continues in today's gospel.
The disciples were all gathered in the upper room
   listening and trying to make sense
   out of these two disciples
   who were telling them about the stranger
   who had walked with them
   on their way to Emmaus and made their hearts burn;
   how they only came to know that he was the risen Jesus
   when they saw him break the bread.

It was in the middle of that chaotic conversation
   that Jesus stood in their midst and said to them,
   "Peace to you."
Who would have ever thought
   that the risen Jesus would have said that?
   "Peace to you."
Wasn't that the greeting Jesus always used,
   even when he was with them in the flesh?
It was the greeting most folks used and still use
   in that part of the world:
   "Shalom."
It was an ordinary greeting,
   an expression of good wishes.
Imagine that your best friend has died.
You are sitting in the family room,
   still grieving, still confused.
Suddenly your friend walks into the room and simply says,
   "Hi, how's it going?" "Hello."
In other words, Jesus greeted his shaky disciples
   with the most obvious,
   the most ordinary greeting in the world: "Shalom."
Now why in the world did the risen Lord do that?

Next, Jesus told them to touch him.
He told them not to be afraid to touch him
   since he was not a ghost.
He was the same Jesus they had kissed many times
   on both sides of the face,
   the way they had always greeted one another
   and still greet one another
   in that part of the world.

He was the same Jesus they had rubbed elbows with
   at the last supper.
He was the same Jesus who often touched them,
   even their smelly fishermen's feet
   which he washed the night before his feet
   were nailed to the cross.
Sometimes, especially when words fail,
   touch means everything.
"Touch me, and see that a ghost
   does not have flesh and bones as I do."
Now why in the world did the risen Lord do that?

Finally, food again.
Jesus can talk until he's blue in the face
   but nobody ever understands.
It seems that only at brunches, lunches and suppers
   did folks begin to understand what he was saying.
In the middle of this extraordinary Easter appearance,
   Jesus asks,
      "Have you anything here to eat?"
Now why in the world did the risen Lord ask that?

You've had a nasty day at work
   and an even nastier one on the road back home.
Your head is spinning.
Tomorrow you *must* do your income taxes,
   and also take your mother who has Alzheimer's disease
   to a nursing home.
But you're also looking forward to going out to dinner tonight
   because, even though it doesn't seem possible,
   tomorrow is your fifteenth wedding anniversary.
In the midst of all this joy and grief,
   half-believing, half-grieving,
   your teenager bursts into the kitchen and asks,
      "Got anything to eat?"

The risen Lord is like a teenager
   who jars us over and over again
   to look at and listen to the obvious.
The risen Lord jarred his disciples with the good news
   that he was not a ghost.
Our faith can never be reduced to a purely "spiritual" realm.

We find the presence of the risen Lord
  in the earthly life of people.

This morning in "that part of the world"
  two million Kurds are starving, shivering, dying.
Why, after everything that has happened,
  are they still strangers to us?
Are we so tied up in our yellow ribbons
  that we can't be Christ to them?
And in "this part of the world" your teenager asks,
  "Got anything to eat?"
Besides food, maybe what she really wants
  is someone to listen to her story.

The risen Lord told his disciples and tells us as well
  that we are not called to be ghost-busters
  but spirit-seekers.
That's what Easter people believe!

19
MESSENGERS OF ENCOURAGEMENT
Fifth Sunday of Easter (B)

- Acts 9:26–31
- 1 John 2:18–24
- John 15:1–8

I've spent a good part of this past two weeks
    reading Martin Luther.
I'm preparing for a presentation that I've been invited to give
    at a Lutheran/Roman Catholic Study Day in Pennsylvania.

Historians today realize
    that Luther's break from the Roman Catholic Church
    came about for many reasons.
Some were theological, some political, some economic.
There are even a few authors who add psychological reasons.

What struck me as I went back to this sixteenth century literature
    was the name-calling that went on back and forth
    between Rome and Luther.
The pope called Luther
    "the wild boar in the vineyard of the Lord."
Luther called the pope the "antichrist,"
    and said that St. Thomas Aquinas had such a "large paunch
    that he could eat a whole goose at one sitting."

Yes, it's true, as the historians tell us,
    there were many reasons for the division
    that came about in the church over four hundred years ago.
But when I pondered all this bitter name-calling on both sides,
    I couldn't help but think
    that this was a story of church people

who refused to let go,
who hung on stubbornly to a church
that in many ways had become a heap of withered branches
instead of a vine bearing the fruit of Christ.

The Easter stories are all about people
who finally get the message.
They are stories of people who let go of old ways,
and are reformed by the risen Lord.

We meet such a person today, Barnabas,
the disciple who pleads with the other disciples
to let go of their old perceptions of Saul
and accept him as a brother in Christ.

Barnabas knew first-hand what it meant to let go.
When he became a follower of Jesus,
he let go of his priestly state (he had been a Levite);
he let go of his name (which had been Joseph);
he even sold his farm and laid the proceeds at the apostles' feet.
Barnabas let go of old ways and was reformed by the risen Lord.

We heard the story from the Acts of the Apostles today
about how reluctant the disciples were
to accept St. Paul as a brother in Christ
because they were afraid of him.
"They even refused to believe that he was a disciple."
Even though they themselves had been transformed
by the risen Christ,
the disciples found it hard to believe
that the same could happen to Saul,
their former enemy and persecutor.
Were they afraid of Saul?
Or were they really afraid to change their old habits
of mistrust, and even hate,
which they still held on to?

That's when Barnabas stepped in.
The name Barnabas, by the way, means
"son of encouragement."
Barnabas tells the disciples not to be afraid.
He encourages them to accept the fact

that just as they had been transformed by the risen Lord,
   so had Paul.
After Barnabas preached that day,
   the early church was never the same.
Now it had its best preacher, St. Paul,
   the apostle of the Gentiles.

The Easter story of Barnabas
   is like all the stories we hear at this time of the year.
They are stories of Easter people,
   who still found it hard to give up
   their old ways of believing and acting.

The risen Lord asked Mary Magdalene why she was still crying
   for an old Jesus she once knew and loved.
   He told her,
   "Do not cling to me that way."

After the resurrection, it was business as usual for Peter.
He was still going out to fish—
   not for people but for fish!

The two disciples were going back to their humdrum old ways,
   to their old town of Emmaus.

And Thomas was never going to change.
He said,
   "You know me; I only believe what I see."
He still clung to his old habit of mistrusting his friends.

But in all these stories
   a messenger of encouragement comes along:
   a Barnabas,
   an angel at the empty tomb,
   a stranger on the road,
   the risen Lord himself.
Someone comes along and reminds the disciples
   that something new and wonderful has happened.
The resurrection is about letting go of old ways
   and believing in the power of God to make all things new.

You and I still have a lot of pruning to do.
Even though we're Easter people,
   we still cling to old prejudices
   about our church and other churches;
   about how it's impossible
   to clean up our environment and save our planet;
   about how the only way to have peace
   is to overpower our enemies with force and propaganda;
   about how we can never give up our addiction
   to alcohol, cigarettes, drugs.

Yes, it's true that we are Easter people,
   but we still cling to old dead branches and habits.
At this eucharist,
   we pray that the Lord will send us
   a messenger of encouragement
   so that we too can let go
   and believe in the power of the risen Lord
   to make all things new.

20
THE NEW STUFF OF THE OLD GOSPEL
Seventh Sunday of Easter (B)

- Acts 1:15–17,20–26
- 1 John 4:11–16
- John 17:11–19

On Wednesday, May 15, we celebrate a birthday.
It's the one hundredth anniversary of the first papal encyclical
   on the pressing social issues of modern life.
The encyclical was called *Rerum Novarum,*
   loosely translated: "New Stuff."
The pope who wrote it was Leo XIII.
He was wise enough to know that some folks in his day
   had a new vision of the way people work and live.

Leo watched as Cardinal Gibbons of Baltimore
   had put his neck on the line
   when he boldly supported the Knights of Labor
   as a union of workers.
He also observed another one of his princes,
   Cardinal Manning of England,
   intervene in the dockers' strike.
Manning was so popular with the workers
   that the dockers carried his picture
   alongside of Karl Marx.
And Leo XIII knew how Karl Marx's idea of a new social order,
   that would abolish the free market system,
   was beginning to change not just the minds
   but the hearts of many people.
And so on May 15, 1891,
   Leo XIII himself took a bold stance.

In *Rerum Novarum*
    the pope stressed the right to private property
    and the workers' rights to form unions
    and to receive a just wage.
He also warned against extreme socialists and other societies
    who were hostile to both state and religion.
What Leo XIII did in *Rerum Novarum* was talk about
    "new stuff"—
    especially that the church was not bound
    to any one form of government.

The church was free to criticize any worldly power
    that ignored the human and spiritual rights of people.
This was a courageous stance on Leo's part,
    because the church
    in many years of its history
    had often sided with kings, queens, and dictators
    who trampled the human and spiritual rights of their people.

To celebrate the one hundredth anniversary of *Rerum Novarum,*
    Pope John Paul II issued his own social encyclical the other day,
    Centesimus Annus,
    in which he strongly supported democratic states
    provided they are grounded in basic human liberties and morality.

There will be many articles and lectures
    by learned theologians this week
    expounding on the new social thought that Leo XIII unleashed
    one hundred years ago.
I have just one little footnote to add about Leo XIII that these
    experts will never mention.
Early in his papacy,
    Leo befriended a stray kitten born in the Vatican.
He made it his companion for life.
When he wrote *Rerum Novarum*
    his cat was curled up in the folds of his robes.
Now, I know many will consider this an insignificant fact.
Because of my cat, you may think that I'm biased.
But somehow I think that little cat had something to do with
    Rerum Novarum.

I'd like to think that one day Leo pondered
   his cat's gift of independence
   even of "the Vicar of Christ."
He thought about how a cat does what a cat has to do,
   not out of fear but out of choice.
You don't own a cat; a cat owns you.
I think that's when Leo XIII got the idea
   that the church, too, should be independent
   of any leader, state, or system of worldly power.
It's only then that the church can preach
   the liberating gospel of Jesus.

It's the kind of independence
   that Jesus prayed for in today's gospel.
He prays to the Father
   that his disciples not be taken from the world
   because God loves the world.
But Jesus also prays that his disciples
   not be chained to the world—
   that is, not be bound to any government,
   any power,
   any worldly system
   that is hostile to God's reign,
   God's plan for people.
Jesus asks in his prayer that his disciples
   be consecrated in truth.
It's only when the church is free,
   not bound to any power,
   that the church can speak the truth of the gospel.

Of course, there are still many Christians, many Catholics,
   who think that there are two worlds:
   the spiritual and the temporal.
They begin to squirm when church leaders
   preach about such new stuff as ecology,
   affordable housing,
   cutbacks in federal assistance to the poor,
   capital punishment,
   racism,
   date rape,
   and the *old* order of bombing nations in order to win the peace.

"Don't bring the world into the pulpit.
Talk to us about religion."

But the central message of Catholic social teaching
    is that the church will not stay locked up in the upper room.
We are not a church of wimps blinded by stained-glass windows
    and choked up in incense.
We are not a church that separates
    the spiritual from the temporal.
We are a church that constantly struggles to transform
    the city of woman and man
    into the city of God.

When the Mount Pleasant section of DC blew up in a riot last week,
    I was shocked to read about and see on the TV news
    two of my former students,
    Fathers Don Lippert and Mark Poletunow,
    dodging flying bottles
    and staggering through clouds of tear gas.
They were trying to restore calm to the community,
    to stop the violence
    (which the church can never endorse in any form).
They were supporting the legitimate claims
    of the Hispanic community.
In class, these two Franciscans seemed docile and mild.
They didn't seem to be the type to get swept up
    in the messy religious business of social justice.
But there they were in the spirit of St. Francis of Assisi
    who had a new vision of the world,
    in the spirit of Leo XIII
    who spoke of a new way for the church
    to engage the world,
    and in the spirit of Jesus who,
    because he spoke the truth,
    was crucified by the "rulers of the world."
If it can happen to Don and Mark, Peter and Paul,
    Leo XIII and John Paul II,
    it can happen to us
    who are still waiting for someone else
    to change the world.

21
LOOKING FOR SIGNS
Second Sunday of Easter (C)

- Acts 5:12–16
- Revelation 1:9–11,12–13,17–19
- John 20:19–31

One of the most exciting days of my life as a kid
   was when my mother announced,
   "Your brother Charlie has the measles!"
I had never seen a kid with measles.
The thought of my older brother covered with little red dots
   tickled my imagination.
And I knew that since I always copied
   whatever my big brother did,
   I, too, would soon sport measles
   and have a few days off from school.
I went up to my bedroom and waited for hours,
   but the measles never arrived.
Finally, I gave up and went downstairs to dinner.
I felt cheated not only because I didn't have measles,
   but because of all those wasted hours I had spent
   looking for them to appear.
But in the middle of the meal,
   my father suddenly pointed to my arm and said,
   "Look, you've got measles . . . better get upstairs to bed."

One my great childhood discoveries was
   that no matter how long
   or how intensely you stare at your arms
   you will never actually see a measle pop out.

97

But as soon as you look away,
    in a split second
    one will appear.
Measles are something like forsythia or magnolia
    or the red bud trees
    that seem to pop out suddenly at this time of year.
No matter how long you stare at these trees
    you will never actually spot a sudden bloom.
It's when you look away
    that blossoms grow.

The disciple Thomas was a realist.
I bet that when he was a kid,
    he, too, stared at his arm to watch his measles appear.
Some people are just like that.
They need more than words or promises.
Thomas missed the risen Lord the first time around.
The other disciples described the scene with vivid detail:
    the locked doors,
    the familiar voice of the Master greeting them with *Shalom,*
    the nail marks in his hands,
    the pierced side,
    the breath of forgiveness.
But, for Thomas,
    seeing was believing.
And what he saw wasn't very convincing.
After all, if Jesus really had risen
    and had appeared to the disciples,
    why were the doors still locked?
Why were they still hiding in the closet
    and not out there in the streets
    proclaiming the good news?

Tradition has been hard on Thomas
    because of his lack of faith.
Some pious preachers have even dubbed him
    a poor community member
    since he wasn't with his brothers and sisters
    when the risen Lord first appeared.
But perhaps what he lacked was not faith in God,
    but faith in the people around him.

Thomas had no difficulty in believing Jesus.
   "My Lord and my God," he cried out.
But he did have a problem believing in his friends.
Thomas wanted more than words;
   he wanted signs.
And so it goes for us as well.

I spotted a grim photo in the newspaper on Thursday
   of some modern day Thomases.
It was a photo of the skeptical residents of Cordova,
   a fishing village in Alaska.
It was a photo of folks listening to Exxon officials
   promising compensation for the harvest losses caused
   by the ten million gallons of oil dumped into the water
   by the Valdez tanker.
One man in the photo held a huge sign which read,
   "Don't believe what you hear."
In a sense, the photo represented us,
   who, like Thomas,
   have a hard time believing in what surrounds us.

Faith is tough:
   faith in anything or anybody;
   faith in leaders who have lost courage and conviction;
   faith in massive and institutionalized falsehood;
   faith in corporations that rob our earth of God's good gifts;
   faith in those who captain our tankers and planes
   while drunk and drugged;
   faith in a church that often comes off unreal
   and out of touch with people's lives;
   faith in people who *say* they love us;
   faith, even in ourselves,
   because we know how wobbly we can be at times.
We all have good reasons to doubt.

Yes, we're Easter people and Alleluia is our song,
   but we're also pilgrim people,
   not quite there;
   and so we sing our Alleluia a bit off-key
   and with some hesitation.
We've heard the words,
   but have not always seen the signs.

At times like this,
    it's easy to be seduced by false religion,
    to believe that the spiritual world is only lived
    beyond the grave
    since this world and those who run it
    cannot be trusted.

We've embraced cynicism with melancholy.
We're like Thomas before the risen Lord's second appearance.
We have forgotten how to discern the power of God
    and the fact that our world,
    our church, our families, our lives,
    are finally subject to God's power.

It's only the risen Lord and those who have risen with him
    who can restore our faith.
We can learn from them how to expect everything from God;
    people can change,
    violence can end,
    the good earth can be restored.
We can learn from them to believe in things
    "both seen and unseen."

The risen Lord was not so much impressed with Thomas
    as he is with us
    who still struggle to believe.
He says of us,
    "Blest are they who have not seen and have believed."
May we not only look for signs of faith,
    but learn to become such signs to one another.

22
LISTENING TO A UNIQUE
AND FAMILIAR VOICE
Fourth Sunday of Easter (C)

- Acts 13:14,43–52
- Revelation 7:9,14–17
- John 10:27–30

It would be fitting to shed some new insight on sheep
    especially in this parish community of Good Shepherd.
But most of what I know about sheep and shepherds
    is what I've read in books.
They are notoriously stupid and smelly—
    not a group with which we'd like to find our identity.

Our lives are not identified
    with sheep and shepherds,
    but with computers, television sets
    and Bell Atlantic car telephones.
John Naisbitt's *Megatrends* reveals that
    the number one occupation was once the farmer, then the laborer;
    but now, in our time,
    the number one occupation is the clerk.
The majority of workers in the U.S.A. are information workers
    paid to process data or information.
Almost half of the U.S. gross national product
    is generated by information-related activities.
We have now a two-class society,
    the information rich and the information poor.
In such a world
    information is power.
Life now consists in acquiring enough information
    to control and predict our world
    so that we can live comfortably and without fear.

101

But the irony of our age is that the very information technology
    that was supposed to liberate us
    has begun to control us.
Maybe that's why our young people are so turned off by school;
    they're forced to acquire more information
    than we old-timers ever had to learn.
Let's face it,
    our new information-based technology has brought us
    neither earthly bliss nor eternal salvation.
In a world with so much available information,
    it's tricky to know just what information
    is central for our lives.
In a world with so many voices
    over so many cables and computers,
    we are beginning to wonder whose voice we should listen to.

Our church, too, struggles to listen to the good news
    within this new world
    of instant information and many voices.
The church's theological debates,
    once heard only in sacred halls,
    are now reported in *Time* and *Newsweek*.
The secret sins of the church's shepherds
    are now featured on *Geraldo*.
Our Father's house contains not only many mansions,
    but many voices:
    Mother Teresa and Mother Angelica;
    Cardinal O'Connor and Father Greeley;
    our bishop and our pastor.
We hear our chief shepherd, John Paul II,
    but still recall
    the voice of John XXIII.
Some people now claim that God is speaking to them directly
    in Lubbock, Texas.
Our Father's house contains many shepherds and shepherdesses
    and it's not easy to listen to them all.

We heard today a snippet from the early church,
    from a time when Paul and Barnabas boldly proclaimed
    the good news.
Even then, there were conflicting voices heard in the land.
Some of the sheep who listened that day in the synagogue

wanted to base their religion
    on their own correct performance and information.
But the people who heard and took to heart
    the good news preached that day
    were those whose religion
    was based on the powerful realization
    that God loved them and all people.
They began to grasp the fact that life is not based
    only on information about God
    but also on an experience of God.
That's why Paul and Barnabas urged their listeners
    "to hold fast to the grace of God."

There were conflicting voices in Jesus' time as well.
Some said he was the Messiah,
    while others doubted the fact.
But Jesus had it easy as a preacher.
His listeners knew all about sheep and shepherds.
And so when he stood up to speak in Solomon's Portico
    on the feast of Hanukkah,
    he didn't have to give long explanations
    about sheep and shepherds.
When the folks from Jerusalem asked him
    to state once and for all
    if he really was the Messiah,
    he fired back that they should know better than to ask.
After all, hadn't they seen for themselves
    the works he had done in his Father's name?
Then Jesus used language and imagery that needed no explanation:
    "My sheep hear my voice.
    I know them and they follow me."
The people knew how flocks of sheep mingled together in the hills
    until the moment each shepherd called out
    to his particular flock
    with a unique voice.
Just as Jesus heard the unique voice of the Father,
    so the disciples of Jesus hear the unique voice
    of the good shepherd.

I am uncomfortable to think of the church in terms of sheep
    because of what I've read about them in books.
But I am convinced that in a world

that places such a premium on information,
and in a church with so many voices,
we need to listen in a new way
to the unique voice of our Shepherd.
The Danish philosopher Kierkegaard reminded us,
"There is no lack of information in a Christian land;
something else is lacking."

We can learn from the old metaphor that Jesus used
and listen intently from time to time
amid all the voices
to the shepherd
who calls out to each one of us
with a still familiar and unique voice.

23
LIFE AFTER DEATH
Fifth Sunday of Easter (C)

- Acts 14:21–27
- Revelation 21:1–5
- John 13:31–33,34–35

(Two events prompted me to dwell on the second reading for this particular Sunday. First, there was the tragedy of the loss of forty-seven sailors in Norfolk, Virginia. Second, about a week before this Sunday, I had a conversation with a confrere, Lowell Glendon, S.S., whose special ministry is spiritual direction. Lowell's father had just died of cancer. Just before his dad's death, Lowell had a long conversation with him about life after death. Lowell asked his father what images of heaven he had. "Not too many," he said. "I haven't heard a sermon about heaven in a long time.")

The poet T.S. Eliot referred to April as
    the "cruelest month" since it mixes "memory and desire."
The poet's words are fitting on this glorious April Sunday
    when we desire nature's new spring gifts
    and remember the loss of forty-seven young sailors of the USS Iowa.
They tossed forty-seven yellow carnations into the Elizabeth River
    in Norfolk on Friday
    while our Governor Baliles said:
      "These are peaceful times
      and we're not used to such a tragedy.
      We do not expect it . . :
      and it leaves us even more saddened."

The wives, parents, children and loved ones
    of our fallen sailors weep and ask why?
They wrestle in their cruel April days with answers to questions

people have been searching for
since the dawn of history:
Is there a meaning to our lives?
Is this all there is?
Does God call us home and why so suddenly?
Is there life after death?
Even for those blessed with the gift of faith,
    this sudden separation from their loved ones
    is a jarring event.
Of all the losses,
    of all the hurts,
    of all the pains we experience in life,
    there is none as strong as death.

In the midst of death, believers take comfort
    only in the embrace of friends
    and in the words of scripture.
They feel the compassionate hugs
    and hear the promising words
    like those of the poet John in today's second reading:
        "This is God's dwelling among the human race.
        God will dwell with them and they will be God's people. . . .
        God will wipe every tear from their eyes,
        and there shall be no more death or mourning,
        or crying out in pain,
        for the former world has passed away."

The reason that we read such scripture texts
    at the time of death
    is that the Bible has notions of life and death
    which are different from our own.
We tend to think of life as the continuing function
    of an individual organism.
We tend to think of death as the end of such functioning.
But the Bible interprets life as a community of meaning
    and death as the act of exclusion from the community.
Our old Catholic notion of the community of saints
    is an echo of the biblical meaning of life and death—
    that for those who desire to believe
    in things both seen and unseen,
    there is the hope of eternal life,

where death is not the last word,
but life goes on forever.

It's unfortunate that the images of the afterlife
which we Christians have used over the years
have been so boring and static:
people sitting at the right hand of God's throne
playing muzak on golden harps.

Again the Bible comes to our rescue
since one of the best images of life after death
comes from the Bible:
the image of the banquet.
I like that image
not just because I like to cook and eat,
but because the image of the banquet means
sitting around the table
with friends and loved ones,
interesting guests and storytellers.
When we invite others to the table,
we invite them to more than a meal,
we invite them into our hearts.

I will never forget the meal I shared with family and friends
after my mother's funeral mass nineteen years ago.
Her sudden death shook my faith
like no other event in my life until that time.
The presence of my family and friends
and the promising words of the risen Lord from scripture at the mass
were a precious comfort to me.
But it was the meal after the mass that I remembered most.
At first, I didn't feel like eating.
But as I sat there and watched my family and friends
eating and drinking,
there was a sudden moment
of God's healing grace,
and I thought,
"This is how it's going to be forever."
And so I began to eat.
The image of the heavenly banquet,
of people sharing, giving and receiving,
reminds us that for God

life is energy,
movement,
friendship.
For God, death doesn't mean the end of life,
but a change in life.
For God, death doesn't mean an ultimate separation,
but the beginning of a new meal.
Like Jesus,
like our sailors,
we will all be changed
and we will all be there one day.

24
HAPPY BIRTHDAY!
Pentecost

- Acts 2:1–11
- 1 Corinthians 12:3–7,12–13
- John 20:19–23

Today many preachers will greet their congregations with
  "Happy Birthday,"
  since Pentecost celebrates the birth of the church
  with the coming of God's Holy Spirit.
But for us this Pentecost is a double birthday
  since we celebrate today the twenty-fifth anniversary of the birth
  of our parish community of Good Shepherd.
Our parish community is a child of the Second Vatican Council.

It was born in 1965 with an exhilarating new rush of the Spirit.
Father Tom Quinlan and the community leaders
  were eager to put into practice
  all the wonderful new inspirations of the council.
The Mission Statement of Good Shepherd
  reads like a page from Vatican II:
  it speaks of a diverse community praying and celebrating;
  it reaches out beyond the doors of a church building
  to the larger ecumenical and secular community;
  it sees its mission accomplished not by tyrannical pastors
  lording it over the people,
  but by a shared parish leadership
  "developing and contributing their gifts."
Good Shepherd's Mission Statement sees its mission
  not in pious terms,
  but in building justice and peace on this earth.

Bishop Keating[1] recently noted that
    "social justice issues, frequently complex and sensitive,
    have been an important part of the fabric of this parish
    in its first twenty-five years."

But we remember on this birthday of our parish community
    that another part of the fabric of Good Shepherd
    has been its struggles and bitter disputes and divisions.
In my ministry as a teacher
    I travel about the country a lot
    and get to know quite a lot of church folk.
Whenever I'm asked what parish I "help out at," people respond:
    "Oh, that's where the pastor rode up the aisle
    in a Volkswagen on Palm Sunday."
Or "Isn't that the church where the pastor
    fired the parish council?"
The divisions and disputes at Good Shepherd
    made national church news.

While some people were thrilled with the new rush of the Spirit
    ushered in by Vatican II,
    others were downright threatened by the newness.
It was in this strange mixture of joy and anguish
    that Good Shepherd Parish was born.

I remember preaching in those days
    at the old Basilica of the Assumption in downtown Baltimore.
I told the story one day in a homily
    of how Pope John XXIII opened up some windows
    in his Vatican apartment
    and said that is what the council is all about:
    letting some fresh air into a stodgy old church.
After mass, an old woman approached me and said that
    when Pope John opened those windows with the council
    "he not only let fresh air into the church
    but some birds as well."

---

[1] Ordinary of the diocese of Arlington.

New birth always brings new tensions and worries.
Just as a newborn child brings
   a new set of problems for a family,
   a newborn church brings
   its own set of tensions for God's people
   to struggle and solve.

Our scriptures today remind us of the divisions that existed
   even in the Spirit-filled infant church.
And, just as in our own church today,
   the divisions weren't about great theological debates
   but about basic human differences
   such as language, turf and power and stubbornness
   to change and to grow.

In our reading from Acts
   we hear how the Jews who had come to Jerusalem to celebrate
   Pentecost
   didn't speak the same language.
They came from as far away as Persia and Egypt and Rome
   and spoke the languages of those nations.
A few weeks ago we read from Acts how the early church
   faced one of its first major divisions
   because of a squabble between
   the Hebrew- and Greek-speaking Christians.

When Paul wrote to the Christians in Corinth
   he was well aware that
   their church was torn apart by factions.
Some Corinthians were puffed up by the importance of their gifts,
   especially speaking in tongues.
The Corinthians thought that their gifts existed for their own glory
   rather than for the service of the whole community.

In both these readings we hear how it is the work of the Spirit
   to build up unity
   amid the diversity that exists in every community.
The early Christians had to face their differences
   and take a deep breath of God's Spirit
   in order to work and pray together as church.

In a similar way, our parish community of Good Shepherd
    has had to face its divisions
    and take a deep breath of God's Spirit
    in order to work in unity to achieve its mission:
    that of "Building Community in the Light of Christ."

We live at a time when there are new divisions
    of hatred and selfishness
    that threaten our larger community.
Even on our college campuses,
    where we have always looked for fresh idealism,
    there are dangerous signs
    of racial and religious bigotry and selfishness.
This nation and this world need to be enlightened
    by communities of love and service.
Let this parish of Good Shepherd continue
    to live up to its mission.
Let us continue to be a vibrant Christian community
    amid all our human differences,
    to let everyone know that all things are possible
    when we allow God's Spirit to blow where it wills.

Happy Birthday!

25
A FEAST TO FEEL
Pentecost

- Acts 2:1–11
- 1 Corinthians 12:3–7,12–13
- John 20:19–23

An old tradition says that
   St. Luke was not only a physician
   but an artist.
In his description of the first Pentecost,
   he is more artist than physician.
Luke describes the coming of the Holy Spirit on the infant church
   with the images of tongues of fire parting
   and then resting on each of the disciples gathered in the upper room.
Luke's story is easy to follow and easy to see.

But as a feast,
   Pentecost is not easy to celebrate visually.
In Advent we see a wreath.
At Christmas we have the crib and the tree.
In Lent we focus on the cross and potted cactus in the sanctuary,
   which remind us of our desert journey.
At Easter we light a splendid paschal candle
   and deck the church with lilies.
But except for the red vestments,
   which symbolize those tongues of fire
   at the first Pentecost,
   there's not much to see on Pentecost Sunday.
It wasn't always so.
In some towns of central Europe
   people used to drop pieces of burning wick or straw

from a hole in the ceiling of the church
in order to represent the flaming tongues of Pentecost.
But this practice was eventually stopped
  because it tended to put the people on fire externally,
  instead of internally
  as the Holy Spirit had done in Jerusalem.

Of course, there is the dove
  which from earliest times was used as a symbol of the Holy Spirit
  because of Luke's description of the baptism of Jesus
  when the Holy Spirit descended upon him
  in the bodily form of a dove.
In thirteenth century France real white pigeons were released
  in the cathedrals on Pentecost Sunday
  during the singing of today's hymn "Come, Holy Spirit."
But this practice too was discontinued,
  because the people complained
  that something other than the Holy Spirit
  was dropping from the rafters.

The symbol of the dove can still be seen in churches today
  on vestments and banners.
I don't know about you,
  but I have never related well to a bird.
The symbol of the Holy Spirit as a dove
  is an ancient part of our tradition,
  but somehow it seems to put the Spirit out of bounds,
  up there in the sky,
  inaccessible to ordinary people like you and me.

Besides Luke's vivid story of the first Pentecost
  we also hear today John's version
  where Jesus shows his disciples his hands and his side
  and then breathes on them
  so that they could catch his Spirit.
It is a reminder that Jesus not only died on the cross,
  but he handed over his Spirit to the church.
We can picture the hands and the side,
  but a breath or gush of wind is not something you see
  but something you feel.

In the Bible, wondrous things began to happen
   when people felt God's breath.
God formed the first creature from the clay of the earth,
   but life came only when he felt God blowing into his nostrils.
In Ezekiel's time, people had become an old bone yard
   until that great day
   when "dem dry bones" felt God's spirit bring them back to life.
It was only when Elizabeth felt the Holy Spirit
   that she was able to cry out in a loud voice to Mary:
   "Rejoice, O highly favored daughter!
   The Lord is with you.
   Blessed are you among women."
And even though Jesus had just been baptized by John
   and was filled with the Holy Spirit,
   instead of going out to preach and heal
   Jesus felt the Spirit drive him into the desert
   where he was tested.
The Spirit blows wherever it wants.

And so the more you think about it,
   maybe Pentecost is not so much a feast to see
   but a feast to feel.
I don't mean feeling in any gushy, sentimental sense
   but feeling in terms of prayer of the heart
   which can unravel our tangled thoughts
   so that we can breathe with God's Spirit.

In many spiritual traditions,
   especially in eastern religions,
   people learn to pray and meditate by feeling,
   by becoming aware of their own breathing.
It's odd, isn't it, that we breathe all the time
   but rarely are aware of it
   except in those terrifying moments when a piece of food
   goes down the "wrong pipe."
We then gasp for air.
We suddenly realize how precious is the gift of breath.

There is one old ritual in some parts of Europe
   that is still celebrated on Pentecost.
People climb hilltops and mountains early in the morning
   of this day to pray.
They call this custom "catching the Holy Spirit."

It is a ritual that says that the gifts of the Holy Spirit
    can only be "caught" in deep prayer.

Our humid weather has passed (for the time being).
Thank God, a gentle, cool breeze can now be felt.
If you get a chance today,
    go climb a mountain or even a little hill
    or just go out on the porch and breathe deeply.
Feel the breath of Jesus in you.
Despite all the scars on the earth, the church, ourselves,
    feel how the Spirit of God
    still continues to breathe life into all of creation
    and to renew our own drooping spirits.
Feel the Spirit of God move
    not just in expected places like church,
    but feel the Spirit of God move wherever it wants
    in surprising places and ways.
After you catch God's Spirit,
    go give it away!

ORDINARY TIME

26
COMING DOWN THE LADDER
Second Sunday of the Year (A)

- Isaiah 49:3,5–6
- 1 Corinthians 1:1–3
- John 1:29–34

Despite the overthrow of its monstrous dictator,
    Romania still roars.
This past week thousands of people shouted down their new leaders
    with demands for the end of communism.
At one point, one of Romania's new vice presidents
    got down on his knees and blessed himself.
It was the only gesture that seemed to assure the angry crowd
    that this would be a new and humane brand of leadership.
One can only hope that the desperate kneeling down
    was more than a gesture.
One can only hope that the new leaders of Europe
    will also be true servants of the people.

It's not easy to kneel down to anyone.
From childhood we are taught to "stand up tall."
And that doesn't just refer to our physical posture.
We live in a world where being king or queen of the hill
    is more than just a game.
It's a way of life,
    especially in a country as powerful and rich as ours.
It's not easy to be humble.
It's not easy to kneel down.
It's not easy to be vulnerable,
    to walk in the shoes of those less blessed.

I have a friend, Dolores Wilson,
  who believes that her vocation in life
  is to come down into the lives of others.
For many years she served as principal
  of the Joseph P. Kennedy, Jr. Institute in DC,
  a school for students with developmental disabilities.
It was that experience that moved her to found Bethlehem House,
  a neighborhood home in northeast Washington,
  where she lives with a group of adults
  who are mentally challenged.
Dolores has struggled these past few years,
  trying to explain to her superiors, her friends,
  her religious community, her family,
  how and why she could live such a demanding life.

When people visit Bethlehem House
  and ask Dolores such questions,
  she usually reaches for a well-tattered book from her bookshelf
  and begins reading from Jean Vanier.
Vanier is a layman
  who left the ivory tower of a university
  to found group homes for people
  whom society considered useless and unproductive.

Dolores is a white-haired wisp of a woman
  with a gentle voice and a soft smile.
But when she reads from Vanier,
  she stirs her listeners
  with the fire of a John the Baptist.
She quotes her favorite lines from Vanier
  which have given her own vocation purpose and drive.
At times you can't tell whether Dolores is speaking her own words
  or quoting her teacher, Jean Vanier,
  whose words have become so woven into her own life of dedication.
    "To serve broken people," she reads,
    "means helping them, as a mother helps her child. . . .
    It means going down the ladder and washing their feet
    as Jesus did. . . ."[1]

---

[1] John Vanier, *The Broken Body: Journey to Wholeness* (New York: Paulist Press, 1988) p. 110.

In our gospel today we meet the prophet John the Baptist
  who had attracted large crowds of followers
  through his powerful preaching.
He became so popular that many of his disciples thought
  he was Elijah come back in his fiery chariot;
  some went so far as to declare that he was the Messiah.

But John's biggest moment came the day that he cried out,
  "Look there.
  Look at the carpenter from Nazareth.
  Look at that gentle one,
  so different from me.
  Look at Jesus.
  He's the one.
  Look at the Lamb of God
  who takes away the sin of the world!"
John remembered the ancient Jewish tradition
  that the Messiah would be found in a hidden figure,
  in a person one does not recognize at first glance.

Jesus called John the greatest of all the prophets,
  but never was John greater than when he came down his ladder
  and recognized salvation hidden in his midst.
  "He must increase;
  I must decrease."

John was not the only one
  to come down the ladder that day.
Jesus also made a humble gesture.
He knelt down to John for baptism.
It was a shocking gesture
  because he who was sinless
  took on the ritual of John the Baptist
  which was a baptism for the forgiveness of sins.

Some biblical scholars have remarked
  that it is extraordinary
  that we find John's baptism of Jesus
  recorded by all four evangelists.

It is extraordinary because,
  when the gospels were written,

the early church was struggling to hold on to the conviction
that Jesus was the sinless Son of God.
Wouldn't the fact that Jesus knelt down for baptism
prove embarrassing?
Wouldn't it confuse the people?

The story of Jesus' baptism by John was kept
despite the fact that it was open to misinterpretation.
The story was remembered and cherished because it told us what
kind of Savior we have.
He is a Savior who emptied himself
and came down the ladder
so that he could enter our real world
where our lives,
as blest as they are,
are often cracked at the corners.
That is what we proclaim in the Creed each Sunday:
"For us and for our salvation
he came down from heaven."

May this eucharist where we meet our God
hidden in the humble forms of word,
bread and wine
strengthen us also to come down the ladder
and to know the joy of discovery!

27
WORDS THAT HURT AND HEAL
Fourth Sunday of the Year (A)

- Zephaniah 2:3; 3:12–13
- 1 Corinthians 1:26–31
- Matthew 5:1–12

In the musical comedy *My Fair Lady,*
    Eliza Doolittle becomes fed up with her speech teacher
    who is trying to get her to talk like a lady.
    "Words! Words! Words! I'm so sick of words!"
Let's face it,
    many times we'd like to join in Eliza's complaint.

We have been told by Madison Avenue
    that it's the image,
    not the word that sells.
We have grown weary of political wizards
    who have tricked us with lovely words
    like "safety net," "peace-keepers" and "apartheid"
    to describe ugly realities.
We have all been hurt by words,
    especially those that promised:
    "I will never leave you."
    "I will always love you."
    "I will never lie to you."
Of all the complaints that followed DC's Mayor Marion Barry's
    drug bust,
    the most poignant came from the young people of DC
    who felt used by the mayor
    because they remembered his glib words:
        "Just say no!"

It's easy to become sick of words.
We might even come to the conclusion
    that words don't matter.
Words are cheap.
Deeds are what matter,
    not words.

But is it all that simple?
Can we so easily dump our trust in words?
I have a hunch that,
    despite the fact that we have all been bruised by bad words,
    we are all, in some way,
    waiting to hear some good words.

Maybe that is why when people today choose their leaders,
    they look not only for strength and competency,
    but leaders whose backgrounds equip them to master words.
Is it just a coincidence that Ronald Reagan,
    Mikhail Gorbachev and John Paul II
    were actors in their youth?
When the people of Czechoslovakia overthrew their communist leaders,
    they turned for new leadership not to a politician
    but to a playwright, Václav Havel,
    whose poetic words have given them
    a new and daring hope.
Yes, it's true that from time to time,
    we do sing with Eliza,
        "I'm so sick of words!"
But it's also true that
    we are people who are hungry for words
    that will lift up our hearts.

That is why, before we come to the banquet of the Lord, the eucharist,
    we listen to the word of the Lord.
After all, we are children of Abraham.
Our faith is deeply rooted in what the ancient Jews called
    dabar.
Dabar was more than just the utterance of a sound.
It was a word that had power,
    a word that brought about a new beginning.
We believe with St. Paul that "faith comes from hearing."

We believe with St. John that
  "in the beginning was the Word."

Sometimes the words we hear in the liturgy
  are about people with odd-sounding names,
  living lives that seem so distant from our own,
  like the prophet of today's reading, Zephaniah.
He is the least known of the biblical prophets.
Zephaniah is mentioned only once
  in the New Testament (Matthew 13:41).
The only reason that the church remembers Zephaniah
  is because of a word he spoke in his day to Israel.
The word was *anawim*
  which means the poor little band of people
  who relied completely on the Lord.
Zephaniah is still remembered because thousands of years ago
  he spoke one word, *anawim,*
  and gave new meaning,
  new life,
  new blessing
  to that name and people.

In today's gospel,
  Jesus takes a clue from Zephaniah
  and reminds us that words matter.
Before Jesus healed,
  before he changed the water into wine,
  before he performed great deeds,
  he spoke words that startled,
  challenged,
  and caused the crowds
  to come back to hear more.

From his vantage point
  on top of the mountain,
  Jesus looked at the people.
Many were poor,
  some were still mourning the loss of a loved one,
  some were homeless,
  others were called odd because
  they didn't buy into greed and hatred.
Jesus looked at all these people

and used one word that nobody had ever called them before:
blessed!
Blessed meant "truly happy."
   "Despite what people call you,
   despite what you might even be tempted to call yourself,
   listen to me."
Jesus said,
   "*I* call you blessed.
   You are blessed because you belong to God's kingdom!"

Of all the wondrous words that Jesus spoke,
   the one that people cherished most
   was when he called them
   blessed.
That one word sparked a revolution of spirit
   and changed the world.
That one word of blessing defied empires
   and defined
   a new people.

When we were kids, we sang a song of defiance:
   "Sticks and stones will break my bones,
   but words will never hurt me.
   When I die,
   you will cry
   for all the names you called me."

The little song was wrong.
Words do hurt.
And while they may not break our bones,
   they break our spirits:
   "You'll never amount to anything in life."
   "You stupid little brat,
   I'm sorry I brought you into the world."
   "Get out of here *nigger, kike, wop, fairy, nerd, cripple.*"

Those are words not worthy of disciples of Jesus.
We who follow him could change the world again
   if only we, too, could learn to call others,
   especially the forsaken among us,
   one word:
   blessed!

28

THE ROAD LESS TRAVELED
Eighth Sunday of the Year (A)

- Isaiah 49:14–15
- 1 Corinthians 4:1–5
- Matthew 6:24–34

Next to my cat, Nickel,
   my best friend is Father Mel Blanchette.
He is a fellow Sulpician priest who is also a psychologist.
He spends most of his priestly ministry
   listening to scores of seminarians,
   priests, sisters and lay persons
   who come to his office in the tower of our seminary,
   Theological College in Washington, DC.

One fine spring day, around seven in the morning,
   while Mel and I sipped coffee
   and had already solved all the problems of the church and world,
   his phone rang.
I could tell from Mel's phone conversation
   that he was trying to settle down one of his overly anxious clients
   who had lost an heirloom ring.
Mel is probably a psychologist because his calm voice
   is capable of soothing a wild and hungry tiger.
He closed the conversation by calmly,
   yet firmly telling the woman:
      "Now just remember one thing:
      it was just a ring!"
When he hung up the phone I couldn't resist telling him:
   "Mel, one day, hopefully many years from now,
   I, too, will call you early in the morning
   to tell you the dreadful news that my cat, Nickel, has died.

There is one thing I strongly advise you:
 do not tell me that day,
  'Remember, Bob, he was just a cat!' "

The little story illustrates, I think,
 the dilemmas we all face from time to time
 in dealing with those anxious moments,
 those panic times
 when we're forced to ask ourselves,
  "What really is important in my life?"
These are the moments which the poet Robert Frost knew about
 when he found that "two roads diverged in a wood"
 and he felt sad that he could not travel both.

Jesus also knew those anxious moments,
 when two roads diverged for him:
 one to superficial glory
 and the other a "road less traveled."
Because he was "one like us,"
 he knew those terrible moments of choice.
Jesus knew what it meant
 to feel the pangs of a divided heart.
But he also knew that you simply cannot serve two masters;
 you simply cannot worship more than one God.
Because he knew what was in their hearts,
 their sincere desire
 to follow God's will and seek God's reign.
 Jesus didn't condemn his disciples for being overly anxious.
Instead, he gently chided them.
He looked at them tenderly and said,
 "O weak in faith."
Jesus knew that they were not wicked unbelievers,
 but disciples who were tempted to panic in a moment of crisis
 and forget what comes above everything else:
 trust in a God who loves us
 as a mother loves the children of her womb.

Jesus never denied the fact
 that a good chunk of life is spent
 worrying about what to make for Sunday dinner.
 ("Chicken Surprise" again?)

He recognized the fact that food, drink, clothing
   and all the other "essentials" of life
   must be grappled with.
His challenge was not
   to deny our physical and psychological needs,
   but to stop us from being gobbled up by all these things.
   ("Remember, it was just a ring.")
His challenge was to remind us
   that we are called to worship only one God
   who loves us not only with a Father's love
   but with a Mother's love as well.
We hear the Mother in Jesus today when he gently asks us:
   "Is not life more than food?
   Is not the body more valuable than clothes?"

We live in a very demanding world.
The anxieties mount and cause many to travel tragic roads.
A few years ago the papers carried a story
   about a girl named Amy.
She was fifteen, and had always gotten straight "A's" in school.
Her parents were extremely upset
   when she got a B on her report card.
"If I fail in what I do," Amy told her parents,
   "I fail in what I am."
The message was part of Amy's suicide note.
Amy was a victim of two themes of *The American Fairy Tale:*
   more possessions mean more happiness,
   and a person who does or produces more
   is more important.

On Wednesday we will have our faces smudged with ashes
   and begin once more the season of Lent.
In a way, Lent is all about asking
   who and what are most important in our lives.
We follow a Jesus who went out into the wilderness for forty days
   to ask the same questions.
One of my favorite authors is the minister, poet, novelist,
   Frederick Buechner.
In his book, *Whistling in the Dark: An ABC Theologized,*
   there are a few lines under the heading "Lent"
   that echo the tender chiding of Jesus in today's gospel.
He asks his readers to consider their priorities in life.

Buechner asks:

"If you had only one last message
to leave to the handful of people who are most important to you,
what would it be in twenty-five words or less?
Of all the things you have done in your life,
which is the one you would most like to undo?
Which is the one that makes you happiest to remember?
Is there any person in the world, or any cause, that,
if circumstances called for it,
you would be willing to die for?
If this were the last day of your life,
what would you do with it?
To hear yourself try to answer questions like these
is to begin to hear something
not only of who you are
but of both what you are becoming and
what you are failing to become.
It can be a pretty depressing business all in all,
but if sackcloth and ashes are at the start of it,
something like Easter may be at the end."[1]

---

[1] Frederick Buechner, *Whistling in The Dark: An ABC Theologized* (San Francisco: Harper & Row, 1988) p. 75.

29
PROVERBS REVISITED
Thirteenth Sunday of the Year (A)

- 2 Kings 3:8–11,14–16
- Romans 6:3–4,8–11
- Matthew 10:37–42

I am not the kind of person
   who takes a book like *War and Peace* to the beach.
I went to Crown Books this week
   for some light, summertime reading.
In the non-fiction section these days, one author dominates:
   a minister from Seattle named Robert Fulghum.
Since early 1989,
   Fulghum's *All I Really Need To Know I Learned in Kindergarten*
   has been on the best-seller list.
His new book, *It Was on Fire When I Lay Down,* is following suit.

Fulghum's success is odd
   because he isn't doing what most authors do
   to get on the best-seller list:
   write sleazy novels
   or books on the great controversies of our time.
Fulghum's books simply seek to offer words to live by.
The wisdom he offered in his first book came from the sandbox—
   sayings like:
      "Share everything.
      Play fair.
      Put things back where you found them.
      Clean up your own mess.
      Don't take things that aren't yours.
      Say you're sorry when you hurt somebody.

Wash your hands before you eat.
Flush."[1]

Another popular author, Rabbi Harold S. Kushner,
    offers the best explanation for Fulghum's success:
        "In a world of complex ethical decisions,
        he cuts through the details and says,
            'At the heart are a few simple rules.
            You *can* be a moral person;
            it's not as complicated as it seems.' "

I agree with Rabbi Kushner.
All of us, young and old,
    know that life has become messy and complex.
It's not easy these days even to distinguish
    the good guys and gals from the bad ones.
We live in a world quite different from the film *Dick Tracy*,
    shot in primary and secondary colors,
    like those from an old Crayola box.
The film is a wonderful escape to a less complicated time
    when you could take sides with
    Breathless Mahoney *or* Tess Truehardt,
    Big Boy Caprice *or* Dick Tracy.
But as soon as we come out of the dark womb of the theater,
    we face life in the 1990s
    which is painted not in primary colors,
    but in many hues.
Is Mandela a saint or a friend
    of the Big Boy Caprices of our time?
Is DC's Mayor Marion Barry a hypocrite
    or a victim of a racist society?
Is the solution to the abortion problem excommunication
    or reconciliation?
The great decisions of our time,
    such as when life begins and when it ends,
    are perplexing even for the "wise nine"
    who sit on the Supreme Court and continue to offer
    5–4 decisions.

---

[1] Robert Fulghum, *All I Really Need To Know I Learned in Kindergarten* (Boston: G.K. Hall and Co., 1985) p. 2.

And so, it's not surprising that in our complicated world
    many have turned to books that offer
    simple, concrete words to live by.
These books are like the ancient tradition of
    the proverbs in the Bible.
All of the proverbs of the Bible
    were meant to cut through the maze of life
    and help us to know that
    wisdom, truth, goodness, moral choices,
    life with God
    are real and attainable by ordinary people.
We find this tradition in today's scripture readings.
Elisha was a holy man known for his predictions and miracles.
He multiplied loaves and brought the dead back to life.
Because of his holy reputation,
    Elisha was on many guest lists.
That's why the "woman of influence" invited him to her house.

This isn't like the other miraculous stories
    we read about Elisha.
It's a tale of ordinary goodness.
It was ordinary goodness
    that left a lasting impression on the prophet.
Her story is remembered in detail.
She didn't just invite him to the house
    but she provided a guest room
    with a bed, table, chair, and lamp.
She wanted the holy man to have some privacy and a good snooze.
The "woman of influence"
    didn't let the complications of her barren life
    get in the way of hospitality.
She not only remembered the hospitality proverb of her day,
    but she lived it out.

Throughout his masterful writings,
    St. Paul had the genius of summing up
    his theological letters
    with concrete, ordinary advice.
We heard one of his proverbs today:
    "You must consider yourselves dead to sin
    but alive for God in Christ Jesus."

And in Matthew's gospel today
   we also heard some words to live by:
      "Those who do not take up the cross and follow me
      are not worthy of me.
      Those who find their lives will lose them,
      and those who lose their lives for my sake will find them.
      And I promise you that those who give a cup of cold water
      to one of these lowly ones because they are disciples
      will not want for a reward."

Jesus didn't just offer these proverbs to us,
   he lived out each one of them.
Jesus doesn't advise us to fall over
   important, powerful people
   but to concern ourselves with the "little ones,"
   which means the ordinary members of the community.
And in the tradition of wise advice,
   Jesus is concrete:
   Give those who are sweating it out in a desert climate
   a cup of *cold* water.

I have heard some sophisticated people look down upon
   a return to the ancient tradition of proverbs.
They have called it "bumper sticker theology."
I suppose they have a point.
After all, we don't want to become simplistic
   in our view of the world.
But I have met a lot of people
   for whom such bumper sticker proverbs
   as "One day at a time"
   or "Let go, let God"
   have radically transformed their lives
   and brought back peace to their souls
   and to those with whom they live.

Each Sunday eucharist we hear from the scriptures
   much more than the sayings we learned in kindergarten.
We hear proverbs and parables
   that can truly help us to cut through the maze.
Are we listening?

30
GIVE IT A REST!
Fourteenth Sunday of the Year (A)

- Zechariah 9:9–10
- Romans 8:9,11–13
- Matthew 11:25–30

On the night of the Fourth of July,
    while we celebrated our nation's freedom,
    the champion of homeless people, Mitch Snyder,
    hanged himself in the nation's capital.
His suicide is wrapped in paradox.
Stubborn and strong for thousands of victims in our society,
    he couldn't find the final ounce of grit
    to help him through the day.
For seventeen years he led an organization called
    The Community of Creative Non-Violence,
    but last Wednesday he chose the ultimate act of self violence.
Mitch Snyder's death is a painful blow
    to the weary in our society
    who once were comforted and strengthened
    by his prophetic gifts.

There were, of course,
    the usual soundbite eulogies for Mitch Snyder.
One of the most revealing
    came from another advocate for the homeless
    who often disagreed with many of Snyder's protest tactics,
    Lutheran pastor John Steinbruck.
"Living and working with the homeless can take its toll,"
    said Steinbruck.
"It means to be immersed in a sea of despair
    and not to have concrete victories.

There is no vacation,
    no days off."

Mitch Snyder somehow sensed that he needed a vacation,
    a break from the violent spiral of homelessness
    that was his constant companion.
In the spring,
    he announced that he would take a leave from his community
    and go on an extended retreat
    at the Trappist monastery in Berryville, Virginia.
"I'm a religious person,
    and from time to time it's important
    to renew our relationship with God," he said.
Mitch said he wanted to meditate and
    "do simple work like breaking bread."

It is not for us to judge the final act of Mitch Snyder
    but somehow I wonder
    if he had taken that break at Berryville
    or had taken a rest *somewhere,*
    and listened to the promptings of his restless heart,
    perhaps he would have been given the energy and the peace
    to carry on.
May he finally rest in peace.

We hear Jesus today tell his followers to take a break:
    "Come to me, all you who are weary and find life burdensome,
    and I will refresh you.
    Take my yoke upon your shoulders and learn from me,
    for I am gentle and humble of heart.
    Your souls will find rest,
    for my yoke is easy and my burden light."

Jesus never minced words about the sins
    of the church people of his day.
But of all their sins,
    the one that seemed to rankle him most of all
    was the fact that the religious leaders had taken away
    precious rest and peace from people's lives.
They told the people that in order to have religious meaning,
    in order to be somebody,

they slavishly had to observe
the details of 613 commandments.
The heaviest burden that ordinary people had to carry
was their religion.

The religious leaders had even twisted the meaning
of their most sacred day,
the sabbath.
Ordinary folk were forbidden to perform
even ordinary acts of charity for those in need.
The sabbath law had become so perversely interpreted
that if a fly landed on your nose,
you were forbidden to swoop it off.
The church leaders of Jesus' day had robbed the people
of the rest and peace
that the sabbath was supposed to offer the weary.

Jesus knew that the sabbath was meant as a reminder
that even when God took a day off from work,
the world didn't fall apart.
God rested on the seventh day
and invited all those who were weary also to rest
and to know that there is more to life than
work and worry,
routine and restlessness.

Originally the sabbath was looked upon like the exodus itself,
which freed the people and refreshed them with new life.
Like the exodus, the sabbath was the great equalizer of all,
great and small,
masters and servants,
people and animals
who were invited to the godlike activity of being at peace.

That is why Jesus fought so hard
to restore this original meaning of the sabbath.
He, who was gentle and humble of heart, put it clearly:
"You were not made for the sabbath,
the sabbath was made for you!"
We need a brand-new appreciation of the sabbath in our lives.
We live in a time where new burdens rob us of the peace of God.
None of us here have lived

the draining and heroic days and nights
of Mitch Snyder.
But I believe that in some respects,
   we have all shared his weariness.

We live in a world filled with gadgets
   designed to make life easier,
   but we spend so much time and energy buying these gadgets
   and then more time and energy finding a place to store them.
Even such a simple task as buying groceries has become a burden.
In a recent cartoon,
   Hilary complains to her mother, Sally Forth,
   that going to the supermarket isn't fun anymore
   because Sally has to spend too much time fussing with her coupons
   and checking out the fat and cholesterol content
   of every item she buys.
We are becoming weary of an advertising empire that offers us
   "Lite Lasagna."
Even the simple pleasures of recreation
   have brought new burdens:
   the right sneaks,
   the most expensive equipment,
   the sure-bet putter.
People these days often return from their summer vacations
   more weary than before they left.

It seems that the more efficient, smart and progressive
   our society becomes,
   the more burdens we have to tote around
   and the less time we have for ourselves,
   for our loved ones,
   and for our God.

Our gospel invites us today to cast aside those burdens
   that are robbing us of our peace
   and begin to rest our restless hearts in God's.
In the words of today's teenager,
   "Give it a rest!"

31
GUEST PREACHER: A FARMER NAMED SETH
Fifteenth Sunday of the Year (A)

- Isaiah 55:10–11
- Romans 8:18–23
- Matthew 13:1–9

(About once a year, I preach the homily in the words of a character from
the gospel story.)

When pastors in some Protestant churches
   take their summer vacations,
    they invite guest preachers to deliver the Sunday sermon.
Last July, you may recall, I resurrected that tradition
   and invited the apostle Andrew to preach the homily.

Our preacher today is not as famous as the apostle Andrew.
But he is a man whom Jesus noticed and then used in a parable.
Allow me to introduce to you this summer's guest preacher:
   a farmer named Seth.

"Thank you, Father Bob.
I am deeply honored to be asked to preach today.
My name is Seth.
I was named after the Seth in the book of Genesis.
He was the son born to Adam and Eve after Cain killed Abel.
He was named Seth
   because he was the new seed who was to take Abel's place.
So you see, it's a darn good name for a farmer to have
   because it means 'new seed.'
Jesus often used such images from nature like seed
   to get across his message.

When Jesus preached and talked about
   how God's reign was in our midst,
   he seldom used abstract language.
After all, he was talking to farmers, soldiers,
   women who made bread,
   and men who cast their nets into the sea.
And so he used all the actions of these people
   in order to talk about God's reign.

Jesus preached the way his ancestors preached.
He used not only the book of scriptures
   but the book of nature to talk about
   how God works in our midst.
He preached like the poet Isaiah who lived in a time
   when people were terribly discouraged
   because they lived in exile in Babylon.
Isaiah used nature to describe God's promises.
Just as the rain and snow came down to water the parched land
   and make it fertile and fruitful,
   so, too, would God's promises be fulfilled
   and they would be led to a land of freedom.

You heard Jesus in the gospel today talk about
   a farmer sowing seeds.
Well, that was *me* he was talking about.
One day Jesus spotted me sowing my spring crop.
It was one of those days when things were getting pretty rough for him,
   when the disciples, the religious leaders,
   even his family were getting him down.
It was at such points in his life
that Jesus often wandered off alone to the shore,
   the desert,
   or the fields.
I was sowing the seed the way my father had taught me.
All farmers in Palestine sowed their seed in this unusual way.
We sowed our seeds *before* plowing the field.
Now we realized that way of planting meant that
   we wasted a lot of seed.
But it also guaranteed us a good harvest.
Since our land had only a thin layer of soil above rocky ground,
   it made sense to us to cast the seed everywhere
   rather than search for deep places.

And so, on this particular gloomy day for Jesus,
    he watched me do what my ancestors had done for generations,
    cast the seed wildly everywhere,
    even among the rocks and thorns.
And that's when I noticed him look at me.
I will never forget how his holy face broke out into a smile.
He never spoke to me.
He just waved his hand, the way that farmers do.
But somehow I knew that I had made his day.
He then went back to the people of his life,
    to those who were faithful,
    to those who were wobbly in their faith
    and to those who were downright hostile to him.
I followed him to a place where I seldom went,
    the lake shore.
There he preached a parable
    about a farmer wildly casting his seed everywhere,
    even in those places where it seemed nothing would grow.
I was so embarrassed.
I kept my place way in the back of the crowd.
I could feel my heart pound and my knees knock
    as Jesus, the Christ,
    compared *me* with *God.*

In this parable Jesus wanted to comfort the people
    the way his ancestor Isaiah had comforted the people of his day
    who were wondering where God was
    in the midst of their trials.
Jesus said that despite the setbacks,
    God was at work and that eventually
    God's kingdom would break through.
God was not like the idols of other gods
    who had mouths but didn't speak,
    who had ears but didn't listen,
    who had hands but never reached out to help.
God was *with* the people and *for* the people
    and would never give up on anyone.
God was like me,
    the farmer who never gave up
    despite the droughts,
    the poor topsoil,
    the rocks and thorns.

After Jesus had finished preaching,
    I ran all the way home.
My wife Miriam was waiting at the front door
    wondering where I had been.
It was unlike me to leave the field in the middle of my chores.
Like an excited schoolboy I told her
    how the Master had compared *me* to *God*.
At first she thought I had been working in the sun too long.
    'Sit down right here, Seth,
    and I'll give you a cool cup of water.'
Well, we sat until the sun went down.
We talked that day as we had never talked before—
    about how our life was good despite all its setbacks,
    how our life was a blessing
    because God was *with* us and *for* us.

But because Miriam was a cautious farmer's wife,
    she thought it best that I never tell my story to anyone else.
'It will be our secret,' she said.
But the other day Miriam finally agreed
    that I should share my story with you.
She agreed that you needed to know
    that God not only notices you,
    but listens to you in the midst of your trials
    and will not give up on any of you.
We thought you needed to lift up your hearts!
Well, thanks for listening to an old farmer."

32

FROM SOLOMON TO SOUTER:
BRINGING TO WORK A MIGHTY HEART
Seventeenth Sunday of the Year (A)

- 1 Kings 3:5,7–12
- Romans 8:28–30
- Matthew 13:44–52

George Bush's selection of an obscure Yankee judge
   for the Supreme Court
   has given the media its summer homework.
An army of reporters has invaded
   the sleepy little town of Weir, New Hampshire,
   where they bombard the locals with questions
   about the solitary David Souter.
They managed to find a former girlfriend
   who swears that while Souter is quiet,
   he's also a nice, ordinary type of guy.
So far the most interesting news I've read about the candidate
   is that he wrote his senior thesis at Harvard
   on another New England judge,
   Mr. Justice Oliver Wendell Holmes.

Justice Holmes was not only gifted with a great mind
   but with a great heart as well.
He was shaped and changed by the personal experiences of his life,
   especially his military service in the Civil War.
He was severely shot through the neck at Antietam
   and heard an army surgeon stand over him and say,
      "I've no time to waste on dead men."
When he was an old man,
   starry-eyed Bostonians would ask the hero about war.
   "War?" Holmes would repeat coldly.
   "War is an organized bore."

He once summed up his philosophy of living when he wrote:
"A person's one and only success
is to bring to his work a mighty heart."

If confirmed, the judgments Judge Souter will have to make
will affect this nation's perspective
about great moral issues
like the right to life, individual freedoms,
free speech and assembly,
and our precious American heritage
of the separation of church and state.
These judgments will require great intellect
but also a mighty heart.

We heard another judge today in the scriptures
pray for an understanding heart
to distinguish right from wrong.
In many ways Solomon was not like
the penny-pinching bachelor, Judge Souter.
Solomon was not only married to the daughter of Pharaoh,
but he had 699 more wives to make life interesting.
Souter drives an old battered car,
while Solomon owned 4,000 chariot horses.
Few remember what Souter has said in the past;
he's left no paper trail.
Solomon's paper trail is legendary.
The Bible says that in his lifetime,
Solomon uttered 3,000 proverbs
and wrote 1,005 songs.

But for all his mighty accomplishments,
like building the temple at Jerusalem,
what folks remember most about Solomon
were his wise judgments in court,
especially the famous case involving two women
who claimed the same child.
In that case Solomon used not only his intellect but his heart.
He proposed slicing the child down the middle,
giving each mother one half.
Solomon discovered the real mother,
the woman who said she'd rather lose the case
than hurt the child.

Wise judgments require not only brain but heart.
Let us pray today that if Judge Souter is confirmed,
    he will be able to bring from his storeroom to the courtroom
    "both the new and the old."
Let us pray that he can demonstrate not only intellect
    but a mighty heart.

Of course, sitting judges are not the only people
    who must make wise decisions.
Every day, it seems, we have to choose
    between right and wrong,
    greed and selfishness,
    honesty and lies,
    people and things.
And once in a while we even have to choose
    between life and death.
Not only judges, but we too are challenged
    to discover our mighty hearts.

That's what Jesus was talking about in the two parables today,
    wise and costly decisions.
In the first parable we find a poor farmer having an ordinary day,
    doing what he's been doing all of his life,
    plowing someone else's field.
Suddenly his plow hits a clump and he thinks,
    "Oh brother, it's going to be another one of those days!"
But the clump turns out to be a buried treasure.
Overwhelmed with joy, the farmer begins to sing,
    "Finders keepers, losers weepers."
He then makes a dramatic decision.
For the first time in his life,
    he throws caution to the wind.
He's a poor man,
    but he sells everything he has to buy the field
    so that he can claim the treasure as his own.

Jesus' second parable is about a different kind of a person.
His life is far from ordinary.
The merchant is like the treasure hunters in our own time
    who spend their entire lives
    searching for more riches and better deals
    that will guarantee them lifelong happiness.

The man in the first parable is Joe Six-Pack.
The man in the second parable is Donald Trump.

But it's important to note that in both parables,
    they stumble on a treasure they never knew existed.
All of his life the merchant was looking for fine pearls.
Note the plural:
    pearls.
But, lo and behold, one day he finds a treasure
    he never knew existed:
    a solitary pearl that is so magnificent
    that he too throws caution to the wind
    and sells all the riches he has accumulated in life
    to buy that one pearl.
In biblical times the pearl was a symbol of wisdom.

And so this parable is about making wise decisions.
Jesus says that this is the way it is
    with those seeking the reign of God.
Each day will bring new challenges to us
    as disciples of the Lord.
Some days what looks like a clump in our way
    can turn out to be a treasure.
There will even be a few days in our lives when we will find
    not only what we have been praying for,
    but what we never dreamed was possible.
And then we have to make the decision
    to accept the answer to our prayers.

In all these cases,
    Jesus invites us to "seize the moment"
    and make our decisions with a mighty heart.
Jesus also tells us in these parables
    that such decisions can cost us a lot.
But they bring us a joy
    that nobody can take from us.

33
JESUS IN BRAZIL
Twenty-First Sunday of the Year (A)

- Isaiah 22:15,19–23
- Romans 11:33–36
- Matthew 16:13–20

Do you remember the little *Maryknoll* magazine?
It is still in circulation.
When I was a boy,
   I was intrigued with the magazine's colorful pictures
   of priests and nuns bringing Christ
   to people who lived in distant, mysterious lands.
Everyone in those pictures looked
   glad to be alive and part of the church.
I imagined it all to be glamorous and rewarding.

This month I got close to fulfilling my boyhood fantasy,
   living with Maryknoll missionaries in Brazil.
As usual, our fantasies are not always on target.
In all of Brazil there is only one Maryknoll priest,
   Father Dan McLauglin.
He lives and works on the east side of São Paulo
   in a community with single and married lay missionaries.

While I was there, four nuns arrived
   to set up another Maryknoll community in the city.
São Paulo is Brazil's largest and economically most important city.
It has a population of eighteen million people,
   the fastest growing city in the world.
Although there are pockets of wealth and beauty in the city,
   most of the people live in poverty.
Many have come to the city from the countryside to find work.

They have been cheated out of their homes and farms
    by wealthy landowners.
The area in São Paulo where the Maryknollers live isn't very pretty.
I can still taste the wretched chemical pollution.
I can still picture the overcrowded trains and buses.
I can still hear the night's howling dogs and the police sirens.
And I can still smell the sewerage water that constantly flows
    down the hilly streets.

But what I will remember most about my stint in Brazil
    is the vibrancy of the people as a church.
One Sunday I went with Dan to the community of St. Joseph the Worker.
Because of the large number of Catholics and the shortage of priests,
    Dan celebrates mass only twice a month in their community,
    while on the other Sundays,
    lay people lead the parish in a communion service.
I have rarely experienced such a powerful community celebration
    of word and sacrament.
Nobody had to cajole the people to sing and pray,
    or even voice their opinions during the homily.
It gave new meaning to the word "participation."
It gave new meaning to the word "eucharist."

I also went to the cathedral where the archbishop of São Paulo,
    Cardinal Arns,
celebrates a 6 P.M. mass every Sunday.
The cathedral was packed with people of all ages.
Again, what impressed me was
    how uninhibited the community was
    in celebrating the eucharist.
The people seemed transfixed
    when the cardinal preached about Jesus calling out to Peter
    as he floundered in the water:
        "Have courage; do not be afraid."
The cardinal spoke not about some ancient tale,
    but of the courage to keep walking in faith
    on the turbulent waters of their lives.

In fact, what distinguishes the church in Brazil
    and other third world countries
    is that often their starting point

is not the Bible or church teaching,
but the actual experience of people's lives.
It is only after people look honestly
   at the sinful social structures
   and the poverty and violence of their lives
   that they can then turn to the scriptures
   and realize that the gospels are about them!
Because the parish structure cannot reach most of the people,
   in many Brazilian dioceses
   the church is made up of small base communities,
   people who meet in their neighborhoods
   for Bible reading, worship and community activities.

Before they read and hear today's gospel about who Jesus is,
   many of the people of Latin America
   will reflect on their lives
   and ask if it is God's will
   that so many people are deprived of work and peace.
Is it God's will that in Brazil only
   sixty-nine percent of the people can read,
   ninety million are undernourished,
   and sixteen million children are abandoned?
Is it God's will that there is more land allotted for cattle
   than for people?
Is it God's will that there is inadequate education,
   no medical benefits and no shelter?
Is this what God wants?

It is only after these questions have been asked,
   and reasons given for the poverty of their lives,
   that the faithful then turn to the scriptures.
It is only then that they give a new name to Jesus of Nazareth.
They call him
   the "Liberator."

In St. Peter's day,
   the names "Son of Man" and "Messiah"
   meant something significant to the people.
They signified the anointed one
   who would deliver Israel from its enemies
   and establish God's reign on earth.
Later on in history,

Jesus would be given other names like "Lord,"
which meant that he was above all the powers in this world.

Because many of the poor in Latin America read the gospels
in light of their lives,
the title for Jesus that makes the most sense to them is
the "Liberator."
Jesus is the one who is able to liberate them
from the domination of colonial powers,
from the foreign debt and rich landowners,
from poverty and oppression,
from violence and depression.

Jesus the "Liberator" evokes a new image of God for the people.
Their God is not content to see them suffer passively.
Their God doesn't bind them
but sets them free from every form of slavery.
Jesus is not a violent, military liberator,
but one who frees them to speak the truth
and walk courageously with a God
who is on their side.

Each generation, each nation, each believer is called to answer
the question of Jesus in today's gospel,
"Who do you say I am?"
I believe that we who are privileged here in the first world
can learn something from our sisters and brothers in the third world
by looking at Jesus in a brand new way
as *the liberator of all.*

34
THE CHURCH OF FATHER GREELEY
Twenty-Third Sunday of the Year (A)

- Ezekiel 33:7–9
- Romans 13:8–10
- Matthew 18:15–20

At some point in his life,
    priest, sociologist, novelist Andrew Greeley
    must have read today's gospel from Matthew
    and decided that it was the most important gospel passage
    in the entire Bible.
It seems that Father Greeley has spent
    most of his priestly ministry
    pointing out the faults of his brothers and sisters in
    the Catholic Church.
He uses as his witnesses
    his sociological data to back up his arguments
    and set things right, once and for all.

For fun reading this summer,
    I tackled Greeley's latest book about the church's problems
    and his solutions to them.
The book is *The Catholic Myth:*
    The Behavior and Beliefs of American Catholics,
    which seeks to torpedo a lot of assumptions people have about
    Catholics.

For example, Greeley writes:
    "As for the pope, the Vatican,
    the National Conference of Catholic Bishops,

your own bishop and his chancery,
    they simply don't matter in your ordinary religious life."[1]
He adds:
    "I intend no disrespect to the Vatican or the NCCB
    or the diocesan curia or the officials in power in these institutions.
    I merely wish to assert that the parish and the home
    are where the religious action is. . . .
    The most important religious influences are local—
    the religious behavior of your spouse
    and the quality of preaching by your priest."[2]

Andrew Greeley can be faulted for his naughty tongue
    and his obvious anti-establishment biases.
But his mischievous style doesn't diminish
    his insights into human behavior.
I believe he's on target when he says that
    "the parish and the home are where the religious action is."

You would never grasp this fact by reading the religion sections
    of *Time* magazine or the Washington *Post*.
Stories there are all about the big guns in the church,
    the pope, Mother Teresa, the new archbishop of Canterbury.
We read about the theological debates among theologians
    and more and more these days,
    about the scandalous behavior of those who lead the church.

We need an Andrew Greeley to remind us
    that those stories really don't present the whole picture.
The church continues to struggle, to minister, to heal and help
    in families and parishes around the world.
We need an Andrew Greeley to remind us that
    it is in parishes like Good Shepherd
    that there is no sign of "loss of faith."
Ninety-eight percent of Catholics believe in God.
A third are members of some kind of religious organization.

---

[1] Andrew M. Greeley, *The Catholic Myth: The Behavior and Beliefs of American Catholics* (New York: Charles Scribner's Sons, 1990) p. 145.
    [2] Ibid.

Twenty-five percent pray more than once a day,
    fifty percent at least once a day;
    ninety percent pray at least several times a week.
Greeley points our that while contributions are down drastically,
    Catholics still have a healthy spiritual life.[3]

Two weeks ago we heard from St. Matthew
    about Jesus giving Peter the important charge
    of the keys of the kingdom,
    with power "to bind and loose."
It was the kind of story one would read in the religious section
    of our newspapers and magazines.
It was a story told with a view from the top of the church.

But today's gospel from Matthew is told from below.
It's about the local church,
    the kind of story that Greeley believes is most important.
The power to declare things "bound and loosed"
    is given not just to the rock,
    but to all the little ones who make up the church.

Today's gospel is about ordinary folk in the early church
    struggling to get along,
    especially with sisters and brothers
    who were less than perfect.
It's a story about how the early church,
    even when it was small in number,
    two or three gathered in the Lord's name,
    was the kingdom of God on earth.

The church is not only bishops excommunicating weak members,
    but husbands and wives,
    mothers and fathers and kids,
    people and priests
    quietly helping one another,
    setting one another loose,

---

[3] Ibid. pp. 146–147.

especially in moments of trial and error.
The church is not only the Sunday eucharist,
    but the table prayers of your family.
The church is not only the church in Rome,
    but this parish community.

Of course, we live in a far more complicated time
    than when Father Peyton said,
        "The family that prays together stays together."
Today's lifestyles bring new stresses on people
    to gather as church.
In three-quarters of our families, both parents work.
The beginning of a new school year brings tough demands of
    schedule juggling.
The most important instruction from parents to children is, "Hurry!"
The secular Ezekiel of our day, Ralph Nader, points out
    that corporations are more important in raising children
    than parents are.
"Who's raising the kids?" he asks.
    "Kindercare is raising them. McDonald's is feeding them.
    HBO and Disneyland are entertaining them."

In such a hectic new world there are many who think that
    the answer to the problem is to tack on more hours
    and more responsibilities to the school,
    to ask the schools not only to serve breakfast
    but lunch as well,
    to teach not only math and English,
    but prayer and ethics.

But today's gospel portrait of a small group of people
    praying and gently correcting one another
    is a gentle reminder that whenever we are gathered
    in our homes, our parish, our community,
    no matter how small we are,
    no matter how weak we are,
    no matter how hectic our schedules are,
    we are the church and so Christ to one another.

35
AFTER APPOMATOX
Twenty-Fifth Sunday of the Year (A)

- Isaiah 55:6–9
- Philippians 1:20–24,27
- Matthew 20:10–16

Conservative columnist George Will is picky about his heroes.
Except for some baseball greats,
    he has a hard time
    praising the accomplishments of the work of others.
That is why he got my attention the other day when he announced
    that the TV mini-series, "The Civil War,"
    which begins tomorrow night,
    is the best use ever made of television.
Will goes so far as to describe the mini-series' director Ken Burns as
    the "Homer of America's Iliad."

For more than a century historians have debated
    the cause of our Civil War.
George Will maintains that about fifteen minutes into Burns'
    eleven-hour series,
    you *see* the answer:
You see a nineteenth century photograph of a black man's back.
It's a bloody map of lash scars.
The photo is a shocking reminder that when the war began
    one in seven Americans was owned by another American.

Over a hundred years have passed
    since this nation's bloodiest war.
Despite all the efforts and accomplishments
    of both black and white Americans,
    despite all of our worthy civil rights legislation,

and despite the church's fierce stance
against the sin of racism,
it continues to raise its ugly head.
The Ku Klux Klan still marches not only in white sheets,
but in pin-striped suits and off-the-rack dresses and
clerical robes.
On the other side of the tracks,
some point out that
when certain black politicians are caught breaking the law,
they blame their troubles not on themselves, but on racism.
They see this lack of responsibility as another form of racism.
The Civil War may have ended at Appomatox,
but remnants of the cause of the war still linger.

Racism lingers in the jokes we tell,
the choices we make,
the friends we keep,
the places where we live,
the candidates we vote for or against.

Indeed the very notion of racism is debated in our society today.
How does one define this sin?
Some claim that only those in the majority,
who rob those in the minority of their rights and dignity,
can truly be called racists.
Others prefer a broader definition.
For them, racism is like the common cold:
everyone—
those in the majority and those in the minority,
those in the church and those out of the church,
those who are rich as well as those who are poor—
is susceptible to the virus.

Whatever definition you prefer,
the sin of racism brings misery to all.
And as shocking and embarrassing as it is,
we must have the courage to look at racism
in light of the gospel.

In today's gospel we hear a parable about
the workers in the vineyard,
and if we are honest,

the story shocks us,
both those in the pew and those in the pulpit.
We recognize that there is a civil war
that rages inside each one of us,
a war between what we profess and what we practice.

This parable bothers us because it reaches deep into our souls,
into those places where we cry out:
"It's just not fair!"
This parable takes us back to our childhood
when our brothers and sisters seemed to get
a bigger piece of cake, a nicer bike,
or a better break than we did.
This parable makes us itch because
it reminds us of those times in our lives
when we were left without a date,
without being picked by the team,
without being chosen by the teacher or the boss.
Yes, there are so many times in our lives when it seems that
"It's just not fair!"

Today's parable also makes us squirm because
it strikes so close to home.
It reminds us of our times,
when certain minorities
like African-Americans and Hispanics and Asians
seem preferred to the rest of us
who have been around since dawn.
"It's just not fair!"

That's why it's important for us to realize that
Jesus first told this parable because people,
especially good, religious people,
were complaining to him that
"It's just not fair!"
The faithful were scandalized that Jesus was so open and accepting
of the "no-accounts" of the day,
like the tax collectors, the prostitutes
and the newcomers to God's reign.
The faithful thought that somehow
religion was a matter of reward.
But Jesus told them "no."

It was not a matter of reward
    but a matter of rejoicing in the fact that
    all are invited to the kingdom,
    the first as well as the last,
    the faithful as well as the "sinners,"
    the old-timers as well as the newcomers.
Jesus told the good people of his day,
    those, like us, who feel the tug of racism in our hearts,
    that our faith cannot be measured by our ways,
    but by God's ways
    because God is more generous, more loving, more forgiving
    than our little minds could ever imagine.

In the next few decades our nation and our church
    will continue to be challenged
    by increasing numbers of "minorities" in our society.
By the year 2020,
    the so-called "new ethnics" will make up
    the majority of Catholics in the United States.
By the year 2056,
    the "average" U.S. resident will trace his or her descent
    to almost anywhere but white Europe.
It will be a different nation and a different church.

We can continue to sing, "It's just not fair!"
The gospel today encourages us
    to sing another tune.

36
CATHOLICS AND JEWS
Twenty-Seventh Sunday of the Year (A)

- Isaiah 5:1–7
- Philippians 4:6–9
- Matthew 21:33–43

There was a trick that we played as kids
　　on the way to the movies.
As we approached the Rialto Theatre in North Scranton,
　　we passed a synagogue.
Some wise guy in the crowd would say to the youngest of us:
　　"Your shoe is untied."
When the kid looked down at his shoes,
　　the rest of the crowd cried out,
　　"You bowed your head in front of a Jewish church!"
We were so Catholic and isolated from other faiths in those days
　　that we didn't even know the term "synagogue."
But somehow we had picked up from our adults
　　the fact that we were number one
　　as far as God was concerned.
Other religions,
　　especially the religion of Judaism,
　　were something not only to be avoided but scorned.

That childhood memory came back to me the other day
　　when I read about the wild debate
　　between the two conservative columnists,
　　A.M. Rosenthal, a Jew,
　　and Patrick Buchanan, a Roman Catholic.
Buchanan, the scrappy graduate of DC's Gonzaga High School,
　　lit the match when he argued that
　　there are two groups who want the U.S. to bomb Iraq:

159

"The Israeli Defense Ministry
and its amen corner in the United States."

That claim proved too much for Rosenthal.
The New York *Times'* columnist accused Buchanan of "blood libel"
    and of stirring up an antisemitic storm in this country.
A torrent of letters from both sides of the issue
    now flood the editorial pages of major newspapers.
Some serious accusations have been from supporters of both columnists.
One of the most startling is the claim that
    Pat Buchanan's alleged antisemitism
    is a natural byproduct of Roman Catholic theology.

One can certainly argue against that claim.
The church officially proclaimed during the Second Vatican Council that
    "neither all Jews indiscriminately (at the time of Jesus),
    nor Jews today,
    can be charged with the crimes committed during his passion.
    It is true that the church is the new people of God,
    yet the Jews should not be spoken of as rejected or accursed
    as if this followed from holy scripture."[1]

Although one can point to such teachings of the Catholic Church
    which officially condemn antisemitism,
    this doesn't mean that Catholics don't harbor in their hearts
    the sin of antisemitism.
Even today,
    the Bible can be used to stir up
    old prejudices and fears about
    our Jewish sisters and brothers.

For example,
    each Sunday our first scripture reading in the liturgy
    comes from the Hebrew scriptures,

---

[1] "Declaration on the Relation of the Church to Non-Christian Religions,"
n. 4, *Vatican Council II: The Conciliar and Post Conciliar Documents,* General Editor, Austin Flannery, O.P. (Northport: Costello Publishing Company, 1975) p.
741.

what we have come to call the Old Testament.
Our last reading is from the New Testament.
This very structure may lead some to conclude that
    only Christians are saved,
    have all the answers,
    and are favored by God.
Today's gospel reading of the parable of the wicked tenants
    gives us another example
    of how we can write off our spiritual cousins, the Jews.
The first part of the parable was a story told by Jesus.
Like any good storyteller,
    Jesus often used exaggerated examples
    in order to hold his listeners' attention
    and get his point across.

In this parable he even uses ugly human behavior
    in order to stress the importance of God's reign.
The point of Jesus' story is not to condemn
    the evil actions of the tenants,
    but to tell his listeners,
        "Look at how these tenants stopped at nothing.
        They even murdered the heir in order to own the vineyard.
        You must be just as determined and committed
        in seeking God's reign."

The second part of the parable was added by St. Matthew.
We might say that the second part of this parable was a homily.
Matthew was using an original story of Jesus
    and applying it to the circumstances of the church in his time.
The preacher Matthew took the original story of Jesus
    and gave it a new twist.
He said that the vineyard was Israel,
    the tenants were the Jewish leaders,
    the slaves were the prophets,
    and the son was Jesus whom they crucified.
Since Israel rejected God who owned the vineyard,
    now it is under new management and belongs to the Gentiles.

Now it's easy to understand,
    especially in a culture where Jews were despised,
    how ignorant preachers and teachers of today's gospel story
    could fan the flames of antisemitism.

After all, they could argue,
  "It's right here in the word of God!"
What we miss is the fact that the challenge of this gospel
  was meant not just for the ancients
  but for us today.
That's the only way we should listen to the gospels.
Jesus challenges us not to be smug in our faith,
  not to reject people because they are not one with us,
  but to be and act like him who welcomed all,
  especially the outcast.

Those who claim that antisemitism springs from Catholic theology
  are wrong.
"Catholic" means that we include everyone in our embrace,
  even those not of our faith.
Catholic teaching clearly condemns antisemitism
  as contrary to the gospel and the teachings of Jesus.

This doesn't mean that antisemitism doesn't fester in Catholic hearts.
But the sin of antisemitism springs not from Catholic teaching,
  but from an ignorance of the teaching.
It also springs from ignorance of the Bible.
And, lastly,
  it springs from our families, our friends, our culture,
  who have handed down their prejudices through the centuries
  in subtle, and not so subtle, ways.

But we must realize that we have inherited
  not just a legacy of antisemitism,
  but an inheritance of grace and power
  that can overcome all sin.
Let that peace,
  which, as St. Paul told us today,
  is beyond all understanding,
  stand guard over our hearts and minds,
  in Christ Jesus.

37
CAUGHT IN THE MIDDLE
Twenty-Ninth Sunday of the Year (A)

- Isaiah 45:1,4–6
- 1 Thessalonians 1:1–5
- Matthew 22:15–21

Read my lips:
some things never change.
The controversy in today's gospel about paying taxes
reminds us that the fiery debate that now rages
between the Congress and the President
is as old as the hills of Palestine.

There's something about government
that leaves us all reaching for our Maalox.
Even a good government, like ours,
that emerges from the will of the people at the ballot box,
is a bothersome bogey man in our lives.
After all, governments, even good governments,
can arrest us, enlist us, and force us
to fill out form after silly form.
But of all the intrusions of government,
the one that is the hardest to swallow is taxes.
Remember what happened when King George decided
to tax the tea of the American colonists?
It was the spark that ignited the Revolutionary War.

There are rumblings of another revolutionary war
now being heard in our land.
The Democrats claim that the rich are not being taxed enough
while the Republicans argue that budget cuts,
not taxes, are the answer.

Weary with the rhetoric of both sides,
   some citizens are beginning to shout,
     "Throw all the bums out of Congress
     and let's have some honest government."

I'm not an economist, let alone a politician,
   but as I listen to the angry voices raised over the issue of taxes,
   I'm reminded of something I learned in psychology class.
It is called "cognitive dissonance,"
   a fancy name for basic human behavior.
Some psychologists tell us that people are capable
   of holding together
   two beliefs that seem to be incompatible.
For example, parents could, on the one hand,
   teach their kids that stealing is a sin,
   but, on the other hand,
   carry home from their workplace
   items that do not belong to them.
Another example might be the American citizen
   who proudly displays the American flag
   on every national holiday,
   yet never takes the time to vote on Election Day.
You get the picture.
We are capable, the psychologists tell us,
   of divided hearts.
I believe cognitive dissonance is one way
   in which we can explain our current budget crisis
   and a lot of other crises that bog our nation down.
We Americans, whether rich *or* poor,
   want services and goods but don't want to pay for them.
We want a big party but don't want to pay the caterer.
We want to build jails for the criminals as long as
   they're not built next door to where we live.
We want to end the sin of segregation,
   but we are unwilling to let a member of another race
   reach for the stars.
We want prayer in the schools,
   but we don't pray in our homes.
We want government to serve us,
   but we're not willing to pay for the services.

Long before there was the term "cognitive dissonance,"
   there was the reality.
That reality is reflected in today's gospel.
The people of Jesus' time were burdened by divided hearts.
As Jews they owed their allegiance to God alone,
   whom they were to love
   with their whole heart, soul and mind.
But their land was occupied by the Romans
   who also demanded allegiance,
   and, worst of all,
   the dreaded poll taxes.

And so the religious leaders of the people
   come to Jesus with the question,
      "Is it lawful to pay taxes to the emperor or not?"
Matthew is careful to tell us that these people
   were asking that question in bad faith.
They were really out to trip Jesus up.
They put him between a rock and a hard place.
If he said it was O.K. to pay taxes to Caesar,
   they would have accused him of blasphemy
   because he accepted Caesar over God.
If Jesus had said that one didn't have to pay taxes,
   the religious leaders would have run to the Romans
   and accused him of trying to overcome the government.
What's a Messiah to do?

Jesus chose to answer their question with another question.
   "Since I don't have any," he said,
   "does anyone of you have a Roman coin used to pay taxes?"
Immediately, someone in the crowd reached into his pocket
   and pulled out a coin,
   a coin with the inscription "Tiberius Caesar,
   son of the divine Augustus, the high priest."
Now Jesus could have been much more blunt when he saw that coin.
He could have said,
   "Well, well, I see that you,
   who are so troubled with the Roman government,
   have no trouble carrying and using its coins."

Instead, Jesus simply said,
   "Give to Caesar what is Caesar's,
   but give to God what is God's."
In other words, Jesus invited his questioners to look honestly
   at their divided hearts,
   at their own "cognitive dissonance."

We come to the eucharist as people often caught in the middle,
   caught between allegiance to God
   and to the gods of our time.
Jesus is still inviting us to examine our divided hearts,
   not to cover them with simplistic slogans.
"Give to God what is God's" means to give, as Jesus did,
   when *he* was caught in the middle.

38
WHAT'S IN A NAME? PLENTY!
Thirty-First Sunday of the Year (A)

- Malachi 1:14–20; 2:8–10
- 1 Thessalonians 2:7–9,13
- Matthew 23:1–12

The other night I had a long phone conversation
   with my niece, Mary Jean.
She's excited about the arrival of her second baby
   at Christmas time.
The doctor, that day, told her to expect another boy.
When I asked what she and her husband, Fred,
   were planning to name the baby,
    I was surprised and a bit amused by her response:
      "We haven't decided for sure,
        but the two names we've come up with so far
        are Kyle Alexander and Tyler Michael."
I couldn't help teasing my niece by asking her,
   "Whatever happened to good old fashioned names
   like those in our family,
   Frank, Charles, or even Bob?"

What's in a name?
Plenty!
Some psychologists tell us that people whose names are attractive
   do better in life than people with awkward sounding names.
The names and titles we give one another
   are a powerful part of our lives.
For the last couple of weeks,
   we've been hearing about a group of people
   whose very name conjures up images

167

of evil, deceit and hypocrisy:
the Pharisees.
Two thousand years after they opposed Jesus,
we still use the word "pharisaical"
to describe a deceitful person.
The Pharisees were a lay group
who stood in opposition to the priestly party,
the Sadducees.
The word "Pharisee" meant "the separate one."
In other words, the Pharisees separated themselves
from other religious Jews
by holding on to a strict interpretation of the law of Moses.
They were so strict that they kept tiny scrolls of the law
in little boxes called phylacteries
which they wore on their arms and foreheads.

Today, biblical scholars point out
that not all Pharisees were mean-spirited and hypocritical
in their religious beliefs and practices.
In Luke's gospel, for example,
Jesus was fond of some Pharisees
and they of him.
In today's gospel from Matthew,
we get a clue of the religious flaw
of those Pharisees who did oppose the mission of Jesus.
They were religious people
who hid behind their names.
They loved to be called Rabbi,
which meant "great one" or "father" or "teacher."
They were so wrapped up in these names
that they forgot what was written in those little boxes
that they wore on their arms and foreheads:
"Only God is the great one, the Father, the Teacher."

When the crowds began to give Jesus names like
"Master," "Rabbi," "Lord,"
many of the Pharisees became threatened.
But Jesus gave them good news.
He told the Pharisees to give themselves a new name,
"Children of the one Father in heaven."

The mission of Jesus was to give people *new names*
   so that they could have a *new identity.*
He gave a new name to the poor, the hungry,
   the sorrowful, the persecuted.
Jesus named them "Blessed."
After he named them "Blessed,"
   they began to act like blessed people.
He gave a new name to Simon the fisherman;
   Jesus called him Peter.
The name stuck.
After the Lord had left them in the flesh,
   Peter remembered that the name Jesus gave him meant "rock"
   and so he began to act like a rock.

Jesus gave an entirely new name to those who followed him.
The followers of a Master were called "disciples,"
   but Jesus called them "friends."
And so, they began to act like friends to one another
   and to all they met.

Since the scholars warn us not to lump all the Pharisees together,
   as if they all opposed Jesus and his mission,
   I would like to think that the day
   Jesus challenged the Pharisees
   not to hide behind their names,
   a good number of them changed
   and began to call themselves
   "Children of the heavenly Father."

We all have names and titles,
   not just religious leaders.
We are doctor, officer, nurse, professor, father, mother,
   the "oldest child" or the "youngest child" in the family.
We are liberal, conservative,
   Catholic, Baptist, Irish, Italian, Mexican.
We are American, Republican, Democrat.

We are people who,
   for better or for worse,
   carry names and titles throughout our lives.

Jesus told the Pharisees of his day
    that there is nothing wrong with the title
    as long as we don't hide behind it
    and keep ourselves from recognizing
    that we are all children of God.

Pope John XXIII was the first modern pope
    to receive a delegation of Jews.
When the Jewish leaders were ushered into the papal library,
    they were apprehensive about what to call the pope.
After all, they were meeting the head of a church
    that in its Good Friday liturgy
    once prayed for "the perfidious Jews."
Pope John sensed their uneasiness,
    and before they had a chance to greet him,
    he held out his arms and said,
        "Welcome. I'm Joseph, your brother."
The pope was not just recalling the story of Joseph
    in the Hebrew scriptures;
    he was humble enough to realize that,
    despite all his new titles as pope,
    he was still Giuseppe Roncalli.

No matter what our title, what our name, what our role,
    the greatest is the one who serves the rest.

39
GOD AND MONEY
Thirty-Third Sunday of the Year (A)

- Proverbs 31:10–13,19–20,30–31
- 1 Thessalonians 5:1–6
- Matthew 25:14–30

Have you ever noticed how so much of the gospel
   is concerned with money?
When Jesus describes God's kingdom,
   he often uses images of coins, inheritances,
   paying back debtors, buying fine pearls
   and settling financial accounts
   in order to make a point.

Today's gospel tells us that
   "to everyone who has,
   more will be given and he will grow rich."
Some preachers have seized upon such scripture maxims
   and have gone so far as to say
   that it is a Christian's duty to grow wealthy;
   a person's wealth is even a sign of God's blessing.
This theology in nineteenth century America
   was known as the "Gospel of Wealth."
At that time a Baptist minister named Russell Conwell
   made a deal with his new congregation
   at the Baptist Temple in Philadelphia:
   as he increased the number of parishioners,
   they would increase his salary.
The deal worked.
Russell Conwell eventually became a millionaire
   and the founder of what is now Temple University.

In today's parable, the master seems as crafty and cold-hearted
as a Wall Street entrepreneur.
He doesn't seem to care that the first two invested in junk bonds;
he's only concerned that they made more money.
As for the poor fellow who hid his master's money
in a hole in the ground,
he's thrown out into the street
with the rest of the dead-beats
who never made it in life.

But we miss the point of all these parables
where Jesus spoke about money and investments
if we forget an important key to unlocking the parables:
Jesus was making comparisons.
Because he was such a good teacher,
Jesus was speaking in a way that people could understand.
He was using a popular art form of his time:
exaggeration.
The more important the lesson,
the more exaggerated the example Jesus would use
to make his point.

And so, he was saying,
"Look at what great length the children of this world go
to hold on to their money.
Look how they will invest, cheat, even kill
to keep and increase their earthly treasure.
But you have a greater treasure:
you are a child of my heavenly Father;
you have a vocation, a purpose in life.
You are worth more than the finest pearl,
more than many sparrows,
more than bins bulging with grain.
If the children of this world are so clever,
so active, so risky
in preserving and increasing their worldly treasure,
why don't you do the same
with your human and heavenly treasure?
Why do you stand there in fear and complacency?
Do something about the gifts I have given you.''

If Jesus preached his parables today,
    he would probably point to the children of this world,
    people like Donald Trump, Charles Keating,
    Leona Helmsley and the Keating Five,
    who seem to risk all for the sake of what is secondary in life.

The other day I read about a woman who risked all
    for what is primary to the Christian life.
In a way, she was like the children of this world
    that Jesus often praised.
Dorothy Day, who founded and worked at New York's Catholic Worker,
    was cunning, relentless, suspicious,
    and above all a hard worker
    at what she considered her vocation:
    to feed, to clothe, to shelter the poor
    and to speak out against the sinfulness of war.

The article I read concerned
    recent clerical rumors about Ms. Day.
They say that the cause for her canonization
    is a serious one in Rome.
What's fascinating is that many of her friends at the Catholic Worker
    seem to object to the possible canonization.
They say that they don't want to walk into a church one day
    and see a statue of *Saint Dorothy Day.*
They say that they wouldn't want to see a plastic Dorothy Day
    standing still.
Such a standing statue would mask the fact that Ms. Day
    was always on the move,
    always relentless for what she considered central to the Christian life.
Dorothy's friends don't want a statue that would radiate
    pious satisfaction
    because she was a saint who was never complacent,
    never satisfied,
    about what was primary to the Christian life.

The gift of the human,
    the Christian life that you and I celebrate in this eucharist,
    must never be taken for granted.
Our daily choices and our daily prayer,
    our daily commitments and our struggles

to renew our lives and our world,
are more important than all the possessions
we have or seek to have.

The human, Christian life
    that you and I celebrate in this eucharist
    cannot stand still.
It involves change and risk,
    headache and heartache.
It's a life worth living for
    and even dying for.
It's a life that shares the Master's joy!

40
DESERT STORM: WHAT DO YOU SEE? WHAT DO YOU HEAR?
Second Sunday of the Year (B)

- 1 Samuel 3:3–10,19
- 1 Corinthians 6:13–15,17–20
- John 1:35–42

(This was not an easy homily to preach. People were caught up in yellow ribbons. The Gulf War affected many people in the parish, since many are in the military or are retired military, and many work at the Pentagon.)

When Desert Shield became Desert Storm on Wednesday night
   we were told by the media
     that everyone was glued to the TV
     or listening to the radio
     to see and hear the bombs bursting in air.
But that myth was suddenly smashed
   by the old silver fox, Walter Cronkite,
   who still has the nerve to tell us
   "That's the way it was."
He told his edgy successor, Dan Rather, and his viewers
   that not *everyone* was listening and watching,
   not *everyone* was involved in or even cared about
   the fact that the dreaded war had begun.

On his way over to the CBS news studio,
   Cronkite looked out his cab window
     and was surprised to see and hear life in the Big Apple
     going on as usual.
"Well, maybe they haven't heard the tragic news yet," he thought.
But then he noticed that his cab driver
   was not listening to the news but to reggae music.

175

He asked the cabby if he'd mind tuning in to the news.
"Why?"
"Don't you realize that we are at war?"
The cabby replied,
   "So what? Are you some kind of a soldier or something?"
Not everyone was listening.
Not everyone was seeing.

The first story from scripture that we heard tonight
   comes from the first book of Samuel;
   it is a book about a tone-deaf tribe
   whose vision was blurred.
It's the story of a people who had forgotten
   how to listen to the Lord's voice
   and feel the Lord's presence in their lives.
They go into battle with the Lord's own ark
   and lose it to the Philistines.
A couple of verses before our story of Samuel and Eli,
   we read about the times in which they lived:
      "And the word of the Lord was rare in those days;
      there was no frequent vision." (1 Samuel 3:1)
Not everyone was listening.
Not everyone was seeing.
But then came Samuel.
He was only a boy sleeping in the temple
   where the ark of God was.
Young Samuel was confused by the Lord's voice;
   he "was not familiar with the Lord."
In other words, Samuel believed in the Lord,
   but at a distance,
   not closely, not intimately.

Samuel thought that his master, Eli,
   had called out in the night.
Eli's eyes "had grown so weak that he could not see."
But the old fox still had spiritual vision;
   he told Samuel that it was the Lord who was calling him.
From that day on, Samuel became his people's conscience
   because of his nearness to God
   and his listening to God's voice.

When the war in the Gulf began,
   President Bush sensed he needed moral help,
   nearness to God.
The president didn't summon the head of his Episcopal church,
   Bishop Browning.
He had already been counseled by his bishop
   concerning the church's stance
   to give sanctions more of a chance
   and to avoid first strikes against Iraq.
Instead, he turned to the Baptist evangelist Billy Graham,
   a minister Lyndon Johnson frequently called upon
   during the Vietnam war
   whenever Johnson needed what he called some "tall praying."

Dr. Graham preached a sermon at Fort Myer Chapel
   that sounded a lot like those
   some Catholic homilists preached this week.
They spoke of the "tragic necessity" of this war,
   drawing from the "just war" theory
   first pronounced by St. Augustine.
But other Catholic preachers,
   like Bishop Kenny of Alaska,
   took their cues not from the bishop Augustine
   but from the U.S. Catholic bishops' own pastoral,
   "The Challenge of Peace."
These Catholic preachers also listened to Pope John Paul II
   who has repeatedly spoken out for negotiations and not war.
The other day he said,
   "In the present circumstances
   a war would not resolve the problems,
   but would only aggravate them."

Across this land this weekend,
   preachers of the gospel will grapple in their homilies
   to state some clear message
   about our involvement in the Gulf War.
Some will argue that it is a time for war,
   that it is a just cause.
Others will claim that it is a time for peace,
   and that only when we learn to make peace
   will the world be safe.

And then there will be those religious leaders
  who are caught in the middle,
  who personally opted for negotiations
  and waiting for sanctions to take place,
  but who now want Saddam Hussein's dangerous menace
  to be crushed.

I believe the best that religious leaders can do at this time
  is to urge people to listen, like Samuel,
  to the voice of the Lord.
I believe the best we can do is to urge everyone to see,
  to "read the signs of the times" in nearness to the Lord,
  to pray for what we Catholics have called
  an "informed conscience."
This is not the time for us to turn to simplistic solutions
  where Arab-looking people are hated and harassed;
  where we think that technology and might
  will solve all our problems;
  where we take glee at the bombing of Baghdad
  as if we were watching a rerun of "Top Gun."

There is a line from an ancient Greek poet (Archilochus),
  "The fox knows many things,
  the hedge-hog knows one big thing."
In our gospel, Jesus asks those desiring to get near to him
  to listen to him:
    "What are you looking for?"
He doesn't give them a homily,
  but an invitation to get close to him,
  to "come and see."
Is the "new world order" that we are looking for
  like the hedge-hog that has only one idea,
  one way of looking at the world?
Or can it be the world order of the fox
  which is willing to accept our world
  as a fragile little planet
  with many ideas, religions, and interests?
As we all pray in this time of peril,
  we must listen
  to the Lamb of God who asks us,
    "What are you looking for?"

41
FACING GOD ALONE
Fifth Sunday of the Year (B)

- Job 7:1–4,6–7
- 1 Corinthians 9:16–19,22–23
- Mark 1:29–39

I didn't look forward to yesterday.
Even though it was a Saturday,
    I had to go to school.
The seminary where I teach
    gathered its faculty for an in-service day
    on revisioning.

Revisioning is a buzz word heard these days
    among church groups and religious institutions.
It's a process,
    similar to what our parish community of Good Shepherd
    went through a few years ago,
    when we drew up a mission statement.
The parish community, through its leaders,
    stood back for a moment
    and revisioned what Good Shepherd should stand for,
    what its mission should be in light of the gospel,
    our Catholic tradition,
    and our particular gifts at this moment and time in history.

In a society hit on all sides
    with burning new demands and problems,
    it makes sense for a community to stand back and ask
    what its real mission is.

The process of revisioning
     or coming up with a communal mission statement
     is not an easy task.
It requires hard work and costly decisions.

The process of revisioning,
     or deciding what the next step should be,
     is not always a community affair.
There are times in life
     when a person stands alone and faces mighty decisions.
Today's scriptures present two men,
     Job and Jesus,
     facing their revisioning,
     alone.

First, there's Job,
     who was the richest and most religious man
     in the land of Uz.
But one day, Job's life was turned upside down:
     he lost all of his livestock, barns, hired hands,
     and his seven sons and three daughters.
If that wasn't enough,
     he came down with the dreaded disease of leprosy.
Job's wife was no help.
She advised him to curse God and then go hang himself.
And then came the advice of four friends
     who offered all sorts of theological and pious reasons
     why all this tragedy was occurring.
"God is just," they said,
     "and doesn't do bad things to good people."
They tried to convince Job
     that even though he was a religious man,
     there must have been something that he had done in life to
     offend God.
Job told them that he had not sinned,
     but the four persisted in their belief.
Finally, Job threw his well-meaning friends out the door.

Sometimes we must stand alone before God.
The book of Job does not conclude with an answer
     to the mystery of suffering.

But at the end of the story,
   Job has experienced God's justice and compassion.
He tells God:
"Until now, I heard about you only from others,
   but now I have seen you and know you as you are." (Job 42:5)

The second solitary figure in today's readings is Jesus.
When preparing for this homily,
   I came across an introduction
   to this gospel of Mark which read:
      "Here Mark pictures for us a typical day
      in the early ministry of Jesus—
      a day with prayer and hard work."
Wrong!
This was not meant by Mark to be a typical day
   in the life of Jesus.
It was an atypical day,
   a day when terrible decisions had to be made,
   and friends got in the way
   of the process of revisioning.
It was a day when choices had to be faced by Jesus,
   alone.

It was the sabbath
   and Jesus had spent the day teaching in the synagogue,
   exorcising a possessed man,
   and healing the fever of Peter's mother-in-law.
When the sabbath ended at sunset and Jesus opened the door
   there was the whole town, bandaged and broken,
   waiting to be healed.
After all demons had been cast out
   and the bodies made whole again,
   Jesus finally went to bed.

But, like Job, he couldn't fall asleep;
   he tossed and turned while the night dragged on.
That's probably why Jesus got up at dawn.
Mark says that "he went off to a lonely place in the desert;
   there he was absorbed in prayer."
Mark's use of the phrase "a lonely place in the desert"
   is a clue that this was not sweet prayer,
   a lovely spiritual oasis after a busy day of work.

Mark used the same phrase,
  "a lonely place in the desert,"
  to describe the place where Jesus encountered
  the temptations of Satan.
This is the kind of prayer where hard decisions are made,
  where there is a battle with demons
  and a solitary look at the face of God.
First, Jesus was tempted by Satan;
  now, he is tempted even by his well-meaning friends,
  like Peter who tells him,
  "Everybody's looking for you"—
  in other words,
  "Stay here in Capernaum
  where you've made such a hit as a wonder-worker."

But Jesus has had a solitary experience
  of revisioning with his Father.
He has come to grips with the terrible reality
  that he has a world to save rather than a town to heal.
He knows the purpose of his life and mission.

The stories of Job and Jesus remind us
  that although our lives are spent with and for others,
  there are those atypical days in our lives
  when we must face our God and ourselves alone,
  and make some hard decisions
  and then get on with our lives.

The good news of today's scripture stories
  is that when that atypical day comes our way,
  God will be there for us.

42

GOD IN A LA-Z-BOY
Eleventh Sunday of the Year (B)

- Ezekiel 17:22–24
- 2 Corinthians 5:6–10
- Mark 4:26–34

For the past month, TV and newspaper advertising
   have pushed Father's Day to the limits.
Have you ever asked yourself
   as you look at these *ad dads*
   why your own father never looked like these GQ models?
The handsome dads of Woody's and Hecht's[1]
   and the svelte continental pops of Calvin Klein
   don't look anything like my father.
Why are they all so young?
Why do these model dads look so fat- and cholesterol-free?
Why are the advertisers trying to convince us
   that dad needs a bottle of Obsession or a Geoffrey Beene shirt
   rather than an electric screwdriver or an ugly tie?
And why in blazes are these model dads so active in the ads?
They're never standing still;
   they're always jogging, playing basketball, tennis.
Where are the old ads where dad is blissfully asleep
   in his new LA-Z-BOY chair?

---

[1] Local department stores.

Maybe what they're trying to do is to change our old perceptions
    about how fathers should look
    and what they *really* want for Father's Day.
Maybe it's all part of the times in which we live
    which some commentators have called *transitional,*
    an "in between time."

I was beginning to think that I was becoming an old fogy
    when my faith in my image of the model dad
    was revived by Johnny Carson in his Friday night monologue.
This is what Johnny suggested would be the ideal gift
    to give to dad on his day:
    make reservations at the finest French restaurant in town
    for the whole family,
    and then let everyone go out to dinner
    so that dad can stay home and have some peace,
    kick back and watch a baseball game on TV.

The gospel we heard from Mark this morning
    has nothing to do with Father's Day
    but, in a way, there is a connection.
Mark also lived in that time of the church
    which could be called *transitional,*
    an "in between time."
The Christians of Mark's time believed in the risen Lord
    but they were also painfully aware
    that the final kingdom of God had not arrived.
They couldn't see any real growth in the church.
They were still being persecuted for believing in the risen Lord.
They were becoming discouraged about the kingdom
    that Jesus had preached.
They looked around at their meager progress and asked,
    "Is this what the kingdom of God is supposed to be?"

That's when Mark looked the people straight in their eyes and said,
    "No, it's not."
    "*This* is what the kingdom of God is."
Mark recalled two parables of Jesus
    which were all about growth.
He told the parable about how the kingdom of God
    is like a man who came home from work one day
    and scattered some seeds in his back yard.

He then came back in the house and stretched out in his
    LA-Z-BOY and had a good snooze.

Matthew and Luke also remembered this parable,
    but Mark is the only one who emphasized
    that the farmer did nothing to guarantee a good harvest:
    no ChemLawn, no Ortho weed killers, no beetle bags,
    and, best of all:
    no watering.
    That's my kind of dad!
Now just because the man stretched out in his LA-Z-BOY
    doesn't mean he was lazy.
He was a good husband and father
    who provided for his family.

What Mark was stressing in this parable
    is that the man was also patient;
    he had learned how to live "in between time."
He also had a great faith in growth,
    that if you wait long enough and believe strongly enough,
    it takes place.
He was a man who had learned to trust
    not just in human efforts
    but in God's good providence.

There are many rich images of God in the Bible:
    God is a king.
    God is a warrior battling for the people.
    God is a shepherd cradling lost sheep in his big arms.
And we should know by now that in the Bible
    God is not always a "he."
    God is also a mother nursing her children.

But today, on Father's Day,
    we catch a unique glimpse of God
    as a Father stretched out in his LA-Z-BOY
    snoozing away.
God is sleeping not because he doesn't care
    but because he trusts us and our own certain growth.
God takes the time to close his eyes and wait.
Like every good father,
    God knows how to let go of his kids.

Just because he sleeps now and then
   doesn't mean he doesn't love us.
Just as when we sleep,
   God's heart still keeps beating;
   his lungs still breathe in and out.
That's our kind of God.
That's our kind of dad.

43
GOD AND GUNS
Fifteenth Sunday of the Year (B)

- Amos 7:12–15
- Ephesians 1:3–14
- Mark 6:7–13

We used to think that the pen
  was more powerful than the sword.
But then, last month, came the sad story of columnist Carl Rowan.
Over the years Mr. Rowan had used his pen eloquently
  to argue against the violence of handguns.
His statistics and reasoning were powerful:
  400,000 handgun deaths in this country
  since the assassination of Robert F. Kennedy.
Most of these involved innocent family members.
The N.R.A. lobbyists challenged Rowan by claiming,
  "Guns don't kill, people do!"
But Rowan was always quick to reply,
  "What kills are people *with* guns!"

But a few weeks ago, Mr. Rowan was startled from his sleep
  in the middle of the night,
  by some frolicking young trespassers
  seeking a cool dip in his pool.
Rowan rushed for his gun and left us with the question:
  Is the gun more powerful than the pen?

I realize that this is a hot debate,
  and I'm sure none of us would have wanted
  to be in Carl Rowan's bedroom slippers that night.
Who knows what we would have done?
What I do find intriguing about the gunshots in Rowan's backyard

is how in the face of fear,
we can all easily give up
even our most cherished principles and beliefs,
and put our trust somewhere else.

Even those of us who bless ourselves with the sign of the cross,
who hold to deep religious values and beliefs,
even we could,
in a moment of terror,
reach not for our faith,
not for our Lord,
but for something else.

Look at what happened to Amaziah, priest of Bethel,
religious leader of his people.
He had become a court chaplain,
telling the king what the king wanted to hear,
trusting more in civil religion
than in the God of Israel.
Amaziah overlooked the unbeautiful people,
who were unjustly treated
because he had reached for faith in the wrong place,
in the human praise and acceptance of the king.
That's why he's so quick
to run the southern rebel Amos out of town:
"Off with you, visionary, flee to the land of Judah."

It's in moments of terror or crisis,
those turning points in our lives,
that we either reach deep down for the hand of God
or we reach somewhere else.

Jesus told the twelve how to trust.
"He instructed them to take nothing on the journey but
a walking stick—
no food, no traveling bag,
not a coin in the purses in their belts."
Those instructions seem awfully drastic, don't you think?
What was the purpose of Jesus sending the twelve out to preach
with so little on their backs,
with not a coin in their wallets?

We do know that there was a pious Jewish custom
    that when people entered the temple courts
    they had to pause to put aside
    their staff, shoes, and money belt.
In other words, all ordinary things had to be set aside
    because they were entering an extraordinary place.
Maybe this is what Jesus was thinking of
    when he sent out the twelve
    so that whenever they entered even the most humble homes,
    they were to enter them as sacred places.
Jesus was telling his followers
    that especially in times of terror,
    when the preaching of the gospel got rough,
    they were to reach out only for God,
    a God who would always be there for them.

Twenty-five years ago,
    the church at the Second Vatican Council
    called itself a "pilgrim people."
One of our Sulpician priests, Father Geno Walsh,
    who refuses to retire,
    agrees that we are a pilgrim people,
    but he says that sometimes
    "we pitch our tents in concrete."
"Traditionalists" give up their most cherished beliefs
    and put their trust in the past.
Some believers put their trust in guns;
    others reach for the horoscope
    or the bottle of drugs that kill.

What about us?
To what or to whom have we turned recently,
    especially when we were afraid?
We come this Sunday to this sacred place
    to receive the word and bread of life.
We come to renew our pilgrim faith in the midst of fear.
We come to reach down for faith in the God
    who walks with us always.

44
TURNING OUR SHOES AROUND
Eighteenth Sunday of the Year (B)

- Exodus 16:2–4,12–15
- Ephesians 4:17,20–24
- John 6:24–35

(The opening story in this homily is taken from William J. Bausch's *Storytelling: Imagination and Faith.*[1])

Many, many moons ago,
   there was a man who had grown weary of his ordinary life.
So one day he decided to leave his hometown,
   his wife and children,
   his ancestral village,
   to search for the
   perfect Magical City
   where all would be new and different and rewarding.
On his journey away from his hometown
   he found himself in a deep forest.
It was dark and so he decided to settle down for the night.
He had a late night snack
   and then prepared to sleep.
The man took off his shoes
   and carefully pointed them to the new direction
   toward which he was going.
However, unknown to him,

---

[1] William J. Bausch, *Storytelling: Imagination and Faith* (Mystic: Twenty-Third Publications, 1984) p. 67.

while he was asleep,
a prankster came during the night
and turned his shoes around.
When the man awoke at dawn
he carefully stepped into his shoes
and continued on to what he thought was
the Magical City.

After a few days,
he came to his Magical City.
But wait a minute.
It was not as large as he had imagined it would be.
In fact, it looked awfully familiar.
He wandered about until he found a familiar street,
knocked at a familiar door,
met a familiar family
and there he lived happily ever after.

There is a sense in which Jesus is always trying
to turn our shoes around.
That's what he's doing with the crowd
on the other side of the lake.
Remember last week,
how the crowd had just eaten the meal
of fish and barley loaves?
Their stomachs were filled
but they were still unsatisfied.
They were looking for something more.
They wanted a more spiritual meal,
something not as ordinary as the fish and barley loaves.
Like the man in search of the perfect Magical City,
this crowd was looking for a Magical Master.
They reminded Jesus how their ancestors were fed,
not with an ordinary meal of fish and barley loaves,
but with a spectacular, spiritual food
that fell down from heaven.

Actually, there is a great irony
about this bread from heaven,
called manna.
Even today, the Bedouins gather manna from the desert ground.
For you see, there is an ordinary explanation for this extraordinary food.

Because of insect damage on the tamarisk trees,
    a sweet sap falls from the leaves.
The sap solidifies during the night and forms the manna.
Think of it this way:
    Manna was one of the original fast foods
    because once the day warmed up,
    it melted away and was lost to the sand.

Jesus turns the crowd's shoes around.
He tells them to stop searching for
    the Magical City,
    the Magical Master,
    the Magical Religion.
He tells them that the real heavenly bread
    is right in front of them,
    in the one they call Rabbi.

There has always been a temptation
    to make religion something magical,
    more than ordinary.
The early church had to condemn some folks as heretics;
    they refused to believe that the Son of God was a man,
    born of a woman.
He was a man like us in all things except sin.
There were times in the church's history
    when some left the Christian community,
    especially when things got too complicated and messy.
They went out to the desert alone to search for Christ.
Now some of these people became saints, but not all.
Those who left for the wrong reasons became losers.

Even in our own day, there is a temptation
    to search for the Magical City.
Some folks are more turned on by the Shroud of Turin
    than by the Christ
    who lives in the person next door to them.
Some are more concerned about the secret letter of Fatima
    than the letter to the Ephesians
    which warns against illusion.
Some even use religion
    as an escape from their duties in life.

There are many reasons why we have a crisis
  with alcohol and drug addiction.
But a key to this problem,
  which robs so many of health and happiness,
  is a quick fix,
  a search for the Magical City
  where all will be perfect.

Jesus is still trying to turn our shoes around.
He is telling us to pay attention to what is under our noses,
  to embrace with gratitude
  the ordinary and imperfect life that God has given us.

Jesus is not the one who brings us a magical grace from heaven.
He is the one who unveils the grace
  that exists in our very lives.
Jesus is telling us today that real religion is not about
  revealing special secrets from heaven
  but noticing, in faith, the mystery
  in our own backyards.
One of my favorite lines of poetry
  is from Elizabeth Barrett Browning who wrote,
    "Earth's crammed with heaven,
    And every common bush afire with God;
    But only he who sees, takes off his shoes."[2]

Jesus tells us,
  "I myself am the bread of life.
  No one who comes to me shall ever be hungry,
  no one who believes in me shall thirst again."
He always turns our shoes around and brings us back home.
That's where God is.
There is no need to search for the Magical City.

---

[2] "Aurora Leigh," *The Poetical Works of Elizabeth Barrett Browning* (New York: Macmillan, 1987) p. 466.

45
IS LIFE REALLY A BITCH
AND THEN YOU DIE?
Nineteenth Sunday of the Year (B)

- 1 Kings 19:4–8
- Ephesians 4:30–5:2
- John 6:41–51

A few weeks ago,
    at a People's drug store,
    I was amused by the advice of a young clerk
    at a check out counter.
After I paid my bill, she boldly said,
    "*Try* to have a nice day."
From the sadness in her eyes,
    it was obvious that she was not having a nice day,
    but was refusing to surrender to defeat.

There are others who are less feisty,
    like the man I saw at the Duron paint store the other day.
He was a large, grumpy looking man,
    wearing an extra large t-shirt.
He, too, was not having a nice day.
From the top of his tousled hair to his Reeboks,
    he was dotted with green paint.
One could only guess what disaster had occurred:
    a false step on a ladder,
    a puppy who overturned the paint can.
Whatever happened,
    the man was depressed and had come back
    to buy more green paint.

His t-shirt was a fit costume for his mood.
It read:
   "Life's a bitch and then you die!"
No doubt you've seen that maxim before
   not only on t-shirts,
   but on bumper stickers and key chains.
It's symbolic, I think,
   of a cynical and depressing attitude in today's society.

What about it? Is it true?
Is life a bitch, and then you die?
What do you think?

One thing is for sure,
   the clerk at the drug store
   and the man in the paint store
   are in good company.
They sit with Elijah under the broom tree and cry out,
   "This is enough, O Lord!
   Take my life, for I am no better than my ancestors."
When Elijah prayed this prayer,
   he was definitely depressed.
He was being thrown out of town by the pagan Queen Jezebel
   for preaching against her false prophets.
He was hiding in the caves,
   trying to determine where to go next.
But even holy people,
   even prophets,
   get depressed from time to time.
This day, under the broom tree,
   was one of those days,
   when life for the prophet was "a bitch."

If we are honest, we have to admit
   that there are times when "everything,"
   as Murphy said,
   "that can go wrong, does."
If you have any doubt about it,
   give a call to coach Joe Gibbs

or the engineers at NASA;
   ask them if they had a nice week.[1]

There are times when,
   despite our faith,
   despite our good will and sunny dispositions,
   things simply get fouled up.
The wallpaper job that you paid big bucks for
   looks hopeless.
Your first young love moves far away,
   or, worse, moves to someone else.
The job promotion that was rightfully due to come your way
   goes to someone less qualified.
The vacation that you had been planning for all year
   turns out to be a dud.
Yes, in all honesty, we have to admit that there are times
   when life truly is "a bitch."

And, of course, the second line of the saying is true as well:
   "Then you die."
Even the people who ate manna in the desert died.
And despite all our fresh fruit and vegetables,
   and aerobics and our marvelous medical advances,
   there will come a day, you can bet on it,
   when a doctor will hold the hand of one of your loved ones
   and say, "I'm sorry; we did the best we could."

I once read a short story of an old couple
   living in the suburbs outside of Paris.
One day, the husband looked at his wife and declared:
   "You know, we have to face it, my dear,
   one of these days, one of us is going to die before the other.
   And I just wanted you to know that, when that happens,
   I plan to move back to Paris."

---

[1] Both the coach of the Washington Redskins and the technicians at NASA
experienced setbacks that particular week.

Even though we hate to admit it
　　and think that only *other* people die,
　　it is true what the man's t-shirt proclaimed,
　　"And then you die."

But lest you think that I have succumbed
　　to the cynicism of today,
　　let me tell you the rest of the story.
As I said, the man was large,
　　and I thought, as I drove home from the paint store,
　　there is room for at least
　　two other sentences on his t-shirt.

Sometimes, life is "a bitch,"
　　but also it could have read that
　　"life is a blessing."
If we concentrate only on the spilled paint cans,
　　the ruined diskettes, the lost loves, the lost ball games,
　　we miss one of the central teachings of our Christian faith:
　　Life is a blessing,
　　a free gift from God.
If we have the guts not to hide our depression,
　　but to seek help and cry out to God
　　even when we are *not* having a nice day,
　　then God will be there for us
　　with food and drink and hope for our journey.

I read a story the other day of a twelve year old boy
　　who fought successfully with the help of medicine and faith
　　to overcome leukemia.
He has written a book for kids about his fight for life,
　　and a TV movie is also being made
　　of his young courageous life.
A reporter asked his mother if the boy's attitude on life
　　had changed since his recovery.
She responded by telling how recently
　　the boy and his older brother had just been defeated
　　by their rivals in a baseball game.
On the way home in the car,
　　the older brother kept pouting about the loss.
The younger brother simply said,
　　"Why are you so down?

We're not bleeding, are we?
We're not in pain.
And, you know, years from now, when we're grown up,
we probably won't even remember this game."
The boy had learned, through pain,
    that life, indeed, is a blessing.

There was room for one more sentence for our friend's t-shirt:
    "Then you rise."
Jesus was bold enough to say that to the murmuring crowds:
    "Let me firmly assure you,
    the one who believes has eternal life.
    This is the bread come down from heaven,
    for one to eat and never die.
    If anyone eats this bread,
    that one shall live forever."

For Christians, the resurrection is more than something
    that happened two thousand years ago.
It happens each time we allow the Father,
    as Jesus did,
    to destroy the evil and depression that rob us of life,
    and to begin again.

So, the next time we see a t-shirt or a bumper sticker that reads,
    "Life's a bitch and then you die,"
    let's not be so self-righteous.
Let's be compassionate and try to understand
    that not everyone is having a nice day.
And then let's whisper a short prayer
    for the depressed in our world,
    that they too may also come to believe that
    "Life's a blessing, and then you rise!"

46
WHY IS JESUS ON THE COVER OF *TIME?*
Twentieth Sunday of the Year (B)

- Proverbs 9:1–6
- Ephesians 5:15–20
- John 6:51–58

During this 1988 presidential campaign,
 Newsweek ran a weekly box article
 called "Conventional Wisdom Watch."
Each week the feature told readers
 what the conventional wisdom was
 about each presidential candidate.
Conventional wisdom is the wisdom
 that *everybody* knows is true.
Another phrase for conventional wisdom is
 common sense.
Conventional wisdom backs up its authority by such phrases as:
 "They say."
 "Everybody knows it."
 "I heard."

There's nothing wrong with conventional wisdom,
 nothing wrong with common sense.
But there is another side to conventional wisdom
 that sometimes gets us into trouble.
It happens when we begin to think our common sense wisdom
 is the same as God's wisdom.
Over and over again in scripture,
 our common sense wisdom is challenged.
Remember what God says in Isaiah:
 "As high as the heavens are above the earth,

so high are my ways above your ways
and my thoughts above your thoughts." (Isaiah 55:9)

The truly wise people in the Bible are the ones
who simply let God be God,
who are open to receive a wisdom higher than their own.
The fool in the Bible is the one who goes it alone
on common sense,
on conventional wisdom,
without God's wisdom.
That's why we hear today in the first reading:
"Forsake foolishness that you may live."
That's why we hear in the second reading today:
"Do not act like fools,
but like thoughtful persons."

One of the reasons the crowd in today's gospel story
could not accept what Jesus was saying
is that they were so tuned in to conventional wisdom,
into what everybody knew was true.
"How could he give us his flesh to eat
and his blood to drink?"
Conventional wisdom,
common sense,
even their religious tradition,
went against what Jesus was saying.
Eating someone's flesh or drinking blood
was strictly forbidden
by the religious laws of the Israelites.
Jesus was giving them a higher wisdom.

Being a follower of Jesus always means that,
while we are to keep our feet on the ground
and follow common sense,
we are also called to accept his wisdom
which often goes against what people think and say.

A good example of what I'm talking about
is our reaction to the controversial new film,
The Last Temptation of Christ.
Regretfully, in the past,
our Catholic response to films that bothered us

was not always smart;
    indeed it was downright foolish.
In 1956, Cardinal Spellman of New York
    condemned the sexy melodrama, *Baby Doll.*
He forbade Catholics to see it.
A meager film,
    starring a not-so-talented actress, Carol Baker,
    went on to become an instant commercial success.
I guess the conventional wisdom there was,
    "If the cardinal is against it, it must be good."
Other films in the past like *Forever Amber*
    or the TV miniseries *The Thorn Birds*
    were denounced by Catholic leaders
    even though they had not seen them.

Maybe we've grown up since then.
I hope so.
Maybe we've become less foolish.
After Bishop Anthony Bosco,
    chairman of the Catholic Bishops' Communication Committee,
    saw *The Last Temptation of Christ,*
he wrote a letter to all the American Catholic bishops
    telling them that, in his estimation,
    the film is "flawed both as theology and as cinema."
But he advised against giving it more publicity through protests.
In his letter, Bishop Bosco said that the film is
    "neither as bad as some people think,
    nor as good as Scorsese thinks."

For the record, it is important to point out
    that the film is not based on the gospels,
    but on the fictional novel of Nikos Kazantzakis.
The author was obsessed by the tension
    between the human and the divine in Jesus of Nazareth.

What seems to upset some Christians most of all,
    even those who have not seen it,
    is that it portrays the human side of Jesus
    a little too graphically.
There have always been Christians who have not been comfortable
    with the fact
    that Jesus sweat,

that he had his bad days,
that he was tempted,
that he was human,
that he was truly like us in all things,
except sin.
These folks prefer a Jesus with a more "divine" look—
more like Charlton Heston than like Willem Dafoe.
Maybe we have emphasized Jesus' divinity so strongly over the years
that some people, like Kazantzakis or Scorsese,
are trying to emphasize his humanity.

We should keep our heads straight over this issue.
Our Catholic tradition is firm
that Jesus was both God and man.
This is the faith we declare each Sunday eucharist in our Creed.
It is a faith that comes from a wisdom
that doesn't make common sense,
but is a wisdom like that of the gospel today
that challenges our conventional wisdom
and brings us into a new life.

We need not join rowdy Christian crusaders to protest the film.
By the way, have you ever noticed
how Christian crusaders become sourpusses?
Our faith is stronger than any film Hollywood could produce.
We need not fear that our Christian world is crumbling.
We need only to have common sense
and be open to a wisdom higher than our own.

In the late 1960s,
I remember a cover of *Look* magazine.
On it was a picture of Father James Kavanaugh
who had written at that time a controversial book called
A Modern Priest Looks at His Outdated Church.
In the lead article of *Look,*
there was a prediction that within twenty years or so,
there would no longer be a Catholic Church.
The irony is that there is still a Catholic Church,
but no longer a *Look* magazine.
So much for conventional wisdom!

This week for an article on the film,
　The Last Temptation of Christ,
　there is a picture of the face of Jesus
　on *Time* magazine.
It is the face of our Lord, who was God and man,
　and who after two thousand years
　continues to challenge our conventional wisdom.
Let's follow him.

47
THE WISDOM OF CALVIN
Twenty-Fifth Sunday of the Year (B)

- Wisdom 2:17–20
- James 3:16–4:3
- Mark 9:30–37

One of these days I'm going to write to the Washington *Post*.
It will be a protest letter.
It will not be about an article I object to
    on the editorial page.
No, my letter will be concerned with a far more serious matter,
    the comics.
What I find so disconcerting is that you never know
    which section of the *Post* will feature the comics.
One day they will be tucked away in the business section,
    another day in the sports section.
On Saturday I had to scout around the real estate section
    to find the comics.

I think that it is some sort of a plot
    designed to keep us from the wonderfully human insights
    of those artists who write the comics.
We adults, who are saddled with the problems of the world,
    who are saddened by its bad news and weary of its problems,
    need a laugh now and then.
We need the zany images of the comics
    to keep our hearts light
    and our heads turned toward hope.

Have you ever noticed how children are often the people
    who have the most to offer us in the comics?
Maybe it's because kids are small

and have to look up
   that they have a unique perspective on life.
Charlie Brown, Lucy, Hilary Forth, Dennis the Menace
   somehow see the world differently from adults.

One of my favorite comic strips is Calvin and Hobbes.
Calvin is a wildly imaginative boy.
Hobbes is his stuffed tiger.
When adults aren't present, Hobbes comes alive
   and is Calvin's best buddy.
This past week, Calvin had been depressed over the earth's
   pollution problems.
He and Hobbes decided to leave for Mars.
Calvin says to his mother,
   "So long, Mom.
   Hobbes and I are going to Mars to live.
   Earth's too polluted."
"Have a good time," she responds.
Calvin has one final request,
   "Say goodbye to Dad for us.
   If I find an interplanetary post office,
   I'll write to you once in a while."
His mother shouts back:
   "Calvin, don't stand there with the door open.
   You're letting in bugs.
   Either stay in or go outside."
In the final block, Hobbes says to Calvin,
   "She didn't seem too choked up about us going, did she?"
Calvin responds to his friend,
   "We should've left a long time ago."

With all his wild imagination and naive responses to his world,
   Calvin has a wisdom his parents have lost a long time ago.
Maybe that's what Jesus meant to tell us
   when he stood a child in the midst of his
   quarreling and ambitious disciples and said,
      "Whoever welcomes a child such as this for my sake,
      welcomes me.
      And whoever welcomes me,
      welcomes not me
      but him who sent me."

In Matthew's gospel, Jesus speaks of his disciples
    becoming like children.
But today, in Mark's gospel,
    he is saying something else:
        "Whoever *welcomes* a child such as this for my sake,
        welcomes me.
        And whoever *welcomes* me *welcomes* not me,
        but the One who sent me."
Four times, the word "welcome."
It is key to this gospel story.

Jesus is telling us to welcome a child
    because, unlike adults,
    a child has nothing to give us.
In other words,
    a child is powerless.
And Jesus identifies with the child.
He says,
    "I too, though your Lord and Master,
    am powerless."

That was a tough message for the disciples of Jesus.
They could accept a Lord of power,
    a Lord of miracles and cures,
    and a Lord of revolution.
But a Lord powerless on the cross
    was not their idea of saving the world.
They could accept a Jesus who was Master,
    but not a Jesus who was servant.

What about us?
Maybe this gospel message is even more difficult for us.
After all,
    we live in a world where we are forced to be number one,
    in sports, in business, in school, in nuclear strength.
We wear power ties, drive powerful cars
    and squawk at anybody who will take away
    one speck of our power.
"Go ahead; make my day."
It's the American way.

Maybe that's the charm of the children of the comics.
They don't have the power of adults,
    but they have a wondrous wisdom.
Maybe that's why we read the comics.

Today's gospel story reminds us
    that there is another kind of power.
It is the power that comes
    when we reach out to those in our midst
    who seem to have nothing to give us.

I'm not a betting man.
But if you pay attention very closely this week,
    I am certain that you will meet a child-like person,
    someone with nothing to give you,
    no influence, no gifts, no power.

Jesus tells us that if we welcome that person into our lives,
    two wonderful things will happen.
We will experience a new kind of power ourselves,
    the power that comes from giving.
And we will be welcoming not just a nobody,
    but a somebody:
    Jesus.

48
MY FRIEND, THE SAINT
Twenty-Ninth Sunday of the Year (B)

- Isaiah 53:10–11
- Hebrews 4:14–16
- Mark 10:35–45

Thursday night our presidential candidates were asked in their debate,
"Who are the heroes in American life today?
Who are the ones that you would point out to young Americans
    as figures who should inspire this country?"
Not surprisingly, the candidates gave as examples of heroes
    men and women of our day
    who came not to be served but to serve.

Frankly, I thought it was one of the better questions asked of
    our candidates.
So much of the current campaign has centered on power,
    on who can beat whom,
    on who is Number One.
Precious little time has been spent
    on how we as citizens of a free and blessed land
    can serve others with the gifts that God has given to us.

There was a time, not so long ago,
    when we as a church told our young people
    a lot of stories about heroes and heroines.
As a kid, I was spellbound by the stories of the lives of the saints:
    the loyal soldier, St. Ignatius,
    forming a new army for Christ;
    the quiet nun, St. Therese,
    growing in holiness by living an ordinary life;
    the daring deacon, St. Lawrence,

burning on a grill of hot coals,
and telling his persecutors,
   "Turn me over on the other side;
  I'm only half-done."
Those were the heroes that the church held out
  for the young people of my day.

But somehow, in our sophisticated post-Vatican II days,
  these heroes of the liturgical calendar seem to fade away.
Their lives, their heroic deeds,
  seem foreign to our world.
Let's face it,
  Michael Jackson has become more powerful
  than Michael the Archangel;
  Sting has become more exciting
  than the North American Martyrs.
I don't know why that happened.
Maybe the church needs to look at some new heroes,
  saints of our own day,
  who came not to be served but to serve.

For this particular youth liturgy,
  I thought I would share with you the story of a saint,
  a hero,
  a martyr,
  not of days gone by,
  but of our own times.
His name is Stan Rother,
  a priest of the diocese of Oklahoma City.
A book has been written about this modern saint.
I have left copies of it on the table at the entrance of the church.
I hope that after mass
  you will have a chance to look at them.

I feel lucky,
  because unlike the author,
  who never had the good fortune to know Stan Rother,
  I went to school with him.
It's strange, but back then in the seminary in the 1960s,
  I never thought of Stan Rother as a saint,
  but as a friend.

There was nothing particularly unique about him;
    he seemed like "one of the guys."

The one thing I do remember
    is that Stan was not the brightest of students.
He worked hard at his studies which didn't come easy to him.
He had already been dismissed from a seminary college
    because he couldn't master Latin.
In those days, you couldn't be a priest
    if you didn't know Latin.
Stan's bishop had given him one more chance at a new seminary.
What I remember most about him
    was his determination not to let his studies
    get in his way of becoming a priest.

In June of 1968,
    after various pastoral posts in his home diocese,
    Stan was appointed to a mission team in Guatemala
    by his bishop, Victor Reed.
The man who couldn't master Latin in the seminary
    went on to learn not only Spanish
    but the difficult Indian Tzuthil dialect of his people.
He even translated the gospels for them into this dialect,
    the first time it had ever been done.
Stan Rother came not to be served but to serve.

Because of his service to his people,
    especially his devotion to the poor and the dispossessed,
    he became a serious threat to government officials.
On July 28, 1981, Stan Rother faced his Jerusalem.
Government hoods broke into his rectory,
    tied him to a chair and tortured him.
Stan put up a tough fight against his persecutors.
Skin was ripped from his knuckles
    and bloodstains were found high on the walls of his bedroom.
But he never cried out for help.
When his kidnapers realized that they couldn't take him alive,
    they shot him twice in the head.

Stan's death, like that of Jesus,
    took place in a particular political context.
We say in the Creed,
    "He suffered and died under Pontius Pilate."

But Stan's martyrdom was a spiritual event.
With heroes like Stan,
    God's Spirit breaks through in our own day
    and reminds us that saints are not something of the past,
    but of the present,
    that real power comes not from being served
    but from serving others.

As Jesus approaches Jerusalem
    and his own death in today's gospel,
    even his closest disciples are still blind
    to what real power is all about.
James and John are still slaves
    to the power-brokers of their time.
They want to be ministers of state
    rather than ministers of the people.
They miss the point
    that Jesus had been hammering away at all these years:
        "The Son of Man has not come to be served but to serve."
Young people today live in a world that says
    that power is not who you are,
    but how you can impress others.
They need not only heroes and heroines,
    but parents, grandparents,
    uncles and aunts
    who will support them in a world that pressures them
    to seek false power.

This past summer, I had dinner with some friends of mine,
    Tom and Vicky.
Tom shared the story of how his son told him
    that he didn't want to go into the successful family business
    which his dad had started from scratch.
Instead, Tom Jr. wanted to become a high school teacher.
Now, everybody knows that no one has ever become rich
    teaching high school.
But that didn't matter to my friend.
    "God has blessed us," Tom said.
    "If we can help our son help others, we will."
I drove home that night thinking,
    "Now there's a father and mother who are real in their faith
    and in their vocation of being parents."

We can't all be Stan Rothers and die serving others.
But we can learn from this hero in the faith.
And we can learn from people like my friends Tom and Vicky
    and live our faith by serving others.
That's a power nobody can ever take from us!

49
WHAT DO YOU NEED?
Thirtieth Sunday of the Year (B)

- Jeremiah 31:7–9
- Hebrews 5:1–6
- Mark 10:46–52

You can usually tell
    when Barbara Walters is coming to the end of an interview.
Suddenly the pushy, tough, and embarrassing questions are over.
Barbara's voice turns sweet.
She then asks the real questions
    of Ronald Reagan or Dolly Parton.
Now often that final question sounds corny,
    like, "If you were a color, what would it be?"
Never mind the silly question.
What she's really asking is,
    "What do you really want from life?"
One of the secrets of Barbara's success as an interviewer
    is that she usually gets an honest answer to her last question.

Last week, we heard Jesus ask two of his closest disciples,
    "What do you want me to do for you?"
They answered,
    "See to it that we sit,
    one at your right and the other at your left,
    when you come into your glory."
Their answer was shallow
    and showed how out of touch they were with Jesus.
In today's gospel, Jesus asks the same question of
    the blind beggar, Bartimaeus:
        "What do you want me to do for you?"
"Rabboni," the blind man said, "I want to see."

Beggars can't be choosers.
They have to ask for what they really need.

This story abounds in meaning.
The disciples are more blind than the beggar.
They prayed out of greed;
    he prayed out of need.

And what about you?
How do you pray?
If Jesus asked you today,
    "What do you want me to do for you?"
    how would you answer?
What do you need?

Before we think of an answer to that question,
    we must consider the kind of society
    in which we ask our questions
    and dream our dreams.
It's a society dominated by marketing strategies
    out to convince us that we need a lot.

It's a society where twenty-seven percent of prime time
    is given to advertisement.
That means we could possibly spend, on an average,
    the equivalent of three solid years of our lives
    watching only commercials.
And what is the relentless message of all these commercials?
Madison Avenue convinces us through fifty billion dollars of advertising
    each year that
        Your hair is too curly.
        Your hair is too straight.
        Your skin is too light or too dark.
        Your breath and your underarms need a spray of mint.
        You are overweight.
        You are underweight.
        You have zits!

Our kids are manipulated to believe that they will be deprived
    unless they get the newest piece of junk for Christmas.
And so our buying habits are mainly motivated by self-loathing,
    not by what we really need.

Maybe that's one of the reasons why
    it's so difficult for us to pray today.
We learn from Bartimaeus that true prayer always begins
    by asking for what we really need.

Not long ago there was a special on NBC called "Teenage in America,"
    a show about some of the problems teenagers face
    growing up today.
Surprisingly, one of those problems was homelessness among teens,
    the fastest growing group among the homeless today.

A homeless young girl, about sixteen years old, was interviewed.
She was asked what she wanted most in life.
"A mansion," she said,
    "with big white columns in the front
    and a swimming pool in the back."
"But most of all," she added,
    "it would have a room that would be my very own,
    with a bed, a lamp, and a closet,
    and maybe even a telephone."

What began as a dream for a mansion
    turned out to be what you and I take for granted:
    our own room,
    with a bed, a lamp, a closet—
    a place to call *home*.

What is it that you want Jesus to do for you?
Why do you come to church?
What is it that you expect from God?
What is it that you want for our world,
    our church,
    our kids,
    our future?

I have a hunch.
If only we could learn to pray,
   both as individuals and as a community,
   not from our greed
   but from our need,
   we could become like Bartimaeus:
   people who are not afraid of what the crowd thinks and says,
   people who can call upon God in tender terms like "Rabboni,"
   people who are not afraid to follow Jesus up the road even though it
   leads to Jerusalem,
   people who can really see.

50
IT'S NOT OVER TILL IT'S OVER
Thirty-Third Sunday of the Year (B)

- Daniel 12:1–3
- Hebrews 10:11–14,18
- Mark 13:24–32

Whenever I go to our local video store,
  I feel a bit like Andy Rooney.
I keep asking myself,
  "Why is that?"
In front of me is this marvelous spectacle of videos
  in alphabetical order,
  but their titles have to be read sideways.
Is this some kind of plot designed to boost the business of chiropractors?
Why do the videos have to be read sideways,
  causing a pain in the neck?
Why is that?
Then there are the people I call "video vultures."
They stand at the table where the returned videos are placed,
  waiting to pounce down on the latest offering.
I ask myself,
  "Don't they have anything better to do with their time?"
Then there is the mystery of mysteries
  overheard in conversations between parents and their kids,
    "No, I don't want you to get that video;
    you've already seen it five times!"
But the youngsters usually win out.
They want to see the film again.
Why is that?
Maybe there *is* an answer to that last question.
Maybe they want to see and hear a story
  where they know how it's going to end.

We live in a world and in a time
  when endings are scary,
  especially for our young people.
Will there ever be a time when there will be
  no homelessness, no poverty,
  no pollution, no deficit,
  no threat of war, no AIDS?
With all the problems in the world,
  young people ask,
    "Will I ever live to a ripe old age?"
    "Will my world end with the horrors of a nuclear war?"

Young people do live in an insecure world
  whose ending is uncertain.
Maybe that's why they're attracted to videos
  where the plot is known,
  where the characters are familiar,
  where the ending is certain.
When we're scared,
  we search for endings.

Throughout the history of God's people,
  whenever times got hectic and people got frightened about the future,
  the prophets would talk in vivid and wild images about the end times.
We call this kind of literature an "apocalypse,"
  which literally means "an unveiling,"
  a drawing back of the veil that hides the future.
We hear this apocalyptic language
  in today's scripture readings.

Fundamentalist preachers have a field day
  with the apocalyptic sections of the Bible:
  a darkened sun,
  a moon not shedding light,
  stars falling out of the skies.
These are striking images to convince a lot of people
  "to get religion."
A familiar saying in many southern pulpits is,
  "The Lord's comin' back to kick butt and take names."

But these scare tactics
  were not what the prophets of the Bible had in mind
  when they talked about the end times.

In times of tyranny,
   when faith was threatened,
   prophets used apocalyptic imagery
   not to scare people into religion,
   but to offer them hope in the midst of trial.
That's why Daniel says,
   "The wise shall shine brightly."
The prophet says that despite the present troubles of Israel,
   God will win out and God's people will be victorious.

When Mark wrote his gospel,
   the early church was drowning in a troubled sea:
   Christians were being fed to lions;
   Jerusalem was besieged by the Roman army;
   Jesus had not returned in glory as they had expected;
   false prophets were predicting the end of the world.
It was a time of terrible fear.

And so Mark reached back to some sayings of Jesus
   and to the tradition of apocalyptic literature,
   not to scare but to comfort his fellow Christians,
   to give them the hope of the fig tree.
He told them that despite their present difficulties,
   God was in their midst
   and they would eventually be victorious.
   "The heavens and the earth will pass away,
   but my words will not."

When I was in graduate school
   I became a close friend of Jack,
   whose father was a fundamentalist preacher.
Jack told me that when he was a kid,
   he would always carefully look out the window
   before he went out to play.
He didn't go out if there were clouds in the sky.
He was too afraid
   that Jesus was going to come riding by on one of those clouds!
His dad's preaching had scared religion into him.

I remember that conversation with Jack
   and how we talked about our adult understandings of
   the end of the world.

We both came to the realization
    that we shouldn't be frightened that God will end the world.
What we're really called to do
    is to bring about the end of the world
    as Jesus did:
    by working for peace and justice,
    by helping all people know that they are loved by God
    and that they have a purpose in life,
    by doing all we can to help those in our society
    who are the most neglected,
    the homeless, the depressed,
    the lonely, the unborn,
    the prisoners,
    the ones most despised and misunderstood.

Yogi Berra once said,
    "It's not over till it's over."
It's true;
    we have a long way to go before
    we bring about God's reign on earth.
We will do it
    not because we're scared,
    but because we're convinced
    that it's the only way to come
    to a great ending.

51
HOPE IN JANUARY
Second Sunday of the Year (C)

- Isaiah 62:1–5
- 1 Corinthians 12:4–11
- John 2:1–12

January is an icebox month.
Gray skies and bitter winds don't lift our spirits.
Our mailboxes no longer bulge with cheery Christmas cards.
January's mail provides the dreaded Visa bill
    and our 1040 forms.
There's not even a Redskins' Super Bowl this January
    to warm our innards.
We know that to be a Christian means to hope,
    but it's hard to hope in January.

I looked about this week for some reason to celebrate,
    to break my blue January mood,
    and I think I found it in an anniversary
    that we celebrate this month.

Thirty years ago, on January 25,
    Pope John XXIII shocked the church
    when he announced that he would convoke an ecumenical council,
    Vatican II, in 1963.
Good Pope John said that the idea of a council came as a surprise,
    even to him.
But he knew that the church needed major changes;
    he was also aware that at seventy-seven years of age,
    he had been elected as an interim pope
    and, therefore, he couldn't do very much by himself.
He felt trapped by the curia.

He once told Cardinal Cushing of Boston,
    "I'm in a bag here."
It was under these circumstances
    that the plan for calling a council occurred to him.
The bishops of the world would help him
    not only by counterbalancing the curia,
    but by deciding better than he could alone
    what was needed to bring a new spirit into the church.
Like St. Paul, whose letter to the Corinthians we just heard,
    John believed in the power of the Holy Spirit
    to rekindle new life
    through all the gifts and ministries in the church.

The curia cardinals were shocked by the announcement.
They protested,
    "We could not possibly get prepared to have a council by 1963."
"All right, then," John responded,
    "we'll have it in 1962."
The rest is history.

We heard this morning from another John
    telling us another story to thaw our January hearts
    and give us hope.
We know that more than any other of the evangelists,
    John was a poet.
And so his story of Cana is filled with poetic meaning.

Miracles for John were not just miracles,
    but signs of something deeper.
John records seven such signs in the first half of his gospel.
Today's changing of the water into wine was the first sign
    that God's power is truly at work in Jesus.

We don't know who the couple was whose wedding Jesus celebrated.
Maybe that's because it wasn't just their wedding,
    but the new marriage between God and the people of God.
Another poet, Isaiah, had dreamed about the day when
    "as a bridegroom rejoices in his bride,
    so shall your God rejoice in you."
For John, Jesus is not just a guest at the wedding,
    he is the bridegroom who has come to make
    a loving and lasting commitment with God's people.

Even the fact that there were six water jars
    had a deeper meaning for John.
For Jews, seven was the complete and perfect number,
    while the number six signified something incomplete.
The six water jars meant
    that Israel's days were running short,
    that a new age was at hand
    when Jesus would do away with the imperfections and restrictions of
    the law
    and bring the new wine of grace which was available to all.

And so we see that
    the more we delve into the deeper meanings of the story of Cana,
    the more we learn who Jesus is
    and what God invites us to do.
The story of Cana is all about newness:
    new wine,
    new grace,
    new beginnings.

The story of Cana is like the story of John XXIII.
New life comes at a time when spirits are drooping,
    when folks are embarrassed,
    old, alone, trapped,
    when the wine has run out.

Listen to the voices of people who are trapped:
    "Ah, why should I vote? It doesn't matter who wins."
    "After all these years, I'm not going to change.
    I guess I was born this way."
An old man sighs,
    "It doesn't matter anymore;
    my life is almost over."
A young girl complains,
    "The same old thing;
    this place is boring."
The cleric laments,
    "Rome isn't going to change.
    I might as well give up."
The husband or wife admits,
    "I guess we're just stuck in a rut."

Tomorrow we celebrate another hopeful January anniversary:
  the birthday of Martin Luther King, Jr.
Dr. King never moaned about the fact
  that the wine of freedom was drying up in America.
He believed deeply in the power of God's grace
  not only to change water into wine,
  but to change hearts of stone into hearts of flesh.
His dream of making a great nation
  even greater and more just
  stirred us to begin to change.

It's been estimated that the new wine at Cana added up to
  one hundred and eighty gallons.
Once again, the poet John was pointing to a deeper reality:
  the grace of Christ is inexhaustible.
There is still time for all of us as individuals,
  as a church,
  as a nation,
  to change and believe in the new wine
  that Jesus still pours out for us.

We follow a Lord who changes things:
  water into wine,
  bread into his body,
  old ways into new life,
  January into hope.

52

FROM NAIM TO TIANANMEN SQUARE
Tenth Sunday of the Year (C)

- 1 Kings 17:17–24
- Galatians 1:11–19
- Luke 7:11–17

The sly old actor W.C. Fields
   told his friends he was a dedicated atheist.
But one day some of his friends
   accidentally stumbled upon the comedian reading the Bible.
"Well, now, why are you, an atheist, reading the Bible?"
Fields replied,
   "Oh, I was just looking for some loopholes."

If we were honest with ourselves,
   we would have to admit
   that we are all looking for loopholes.
Even those of us who follow Jesus as Lord
   can become quite clever in setting limits to our following,
   in looking for loopholes in the scriptures.
But each Sunday we gather as a community to meet a Lord
   who challenges our loopholes with stinging clarity.
This Sunday is no exception.

Luke paints a masterpiece for us today
   in the story of the widow of Naim.
Two large crowds meet at the gate of the city:
   one following the dead,
   one following the Lord of Life.
The first crowd is leaving the city
   to go to the place of the dead.

The crowd that follows Jesus is coming into the city,
   the place of the living.
The widow represents the poorest of the poor.
She has lost her only breadwinner.
She is now at the mercy of her friends.
But she wonders as she marches slowly behind her dear son's coffin,
   "How long will they stick around?"
"After the funeral hymns are sung,
   after the crying and the beating of breasts,
   after the meal,"
   she wonders,
   "will they too be gone?"

It's at the gate of the city,
   where death and life meet,
   that Jesus is moved to pity.
Unlike so many,
   the blind, the tormented, the abandoned
   who cried out to Jesus,
   this widow simply cries.
Her tears are enough for the Savior.
Jesus gives the son back to his mother.
Life is restored not only to the son and his mother,
   but to the two crowds
   who now become one:
   "Fear seized them *all* and *they* began to praise God."

In these past few weeks the world has been stunned
   by the huge crowds gathered at Tiananmen Square:
   the peaceful demonstrations of the university students,
   the workers who joined them in their demands for democracy,
   the solitary protester defying a convoy of tanks with sheer grit,
   the massacre of people with tanks and AK-47 rifles.

Something is happening in the communist world
   that even the experts had not anticipated.
At the beginning of the demonstrations in the square,
   a reporter asked one of the students,
     "What is democracy?"
The student replied,
     "We don't know exactly what it is,
     but we want more of it."

The protesters came into the city,
   into the center of Beijing,
   into the give and take of history
   where people seek healing for their hurts
   in struggle and dialogue.
But their leaders responded not by hearing their cries,
   but by fleeing the city to choose death
   for their own people.

At the center of Marxism is a huge loophole.
Marxism lacks spirit.
And because it lacks spirit,
   it offers no compassion and hope.
The individual is unimportant.
Marxism lacks faith in the give and take of history
   where people can choose their own destiny.

No matter how long and hard we read the Bible,
   there is no loophole there.
Jesus, who meets death at the gate of the city,
   responds in compassion with new life and hope.
Even when they rejected Jesus and threw him out of the city
   and left him dead in the Valley of the Skulls,
   he marched back into the city alive
   to be *with* and *for* others.
Jesus is the presence of God who tells us by his actions
   that salvation and meaning are not separate from individuals,
   from history,
   from this world.

It is said that the saintly Gandhi also searched the Bible
   and admitted that he could find no loopholes.
"O Christians, I love your Christ," he said;
   "why are you so unlike him?"
The devout Hindu tried to tell us
   that it is not enough for us to follow the Savior;
   we must be like our Savior to our world.
I believe that the biggest loophole in our Christian lives
   is the belief that we can live for ourselves alone,
   without concern,
   without involvement,
   without compassion for others,
   especially for those who are different from ourselves.

The other day I overheard a man say,
    "I'm tired seeing all this stuff from China every night on TV."
He doesn't realize that this is the first time in history
    that a civil war could break out
    in a country with nuclear arms,
    which could have devastating results for our planet.
It's as if he has never come to grips with the fact
    that we are all sisters and brothers on this earth,
    all connected.
What happens in Tiananmen Square,
    in the rain forests of Brazil,
    in the voting booths of Prague,
    in the executive offices of Wall Street,
    affects us all.
This earth is the only one that God has given us
    in which to meet salvation.

Now there are some religious people who confine holiness,
    meaning,
    happiness,
    to a stained-glass window world
    where we can find our salvation alone with Jesus
    rather than with and through the give and take
    of living with each other.
Mother Teresa once told the story
    of how a group of American professors
    came to the city of Calcutta
    to find the meaning of holiness.
Before they left, they said to her,
    "Tell us something that will help us to become holy."
Mother Teresa replied,
    "Smile at each other."

While there is no loophole in the gospel,
    there is often a loophole in our Christian lives.
Being a Christian means more than knowing the Savior.
It means being a savior like Jesus
    to those at the gate of the city
    who are tempted to choose death rather than life.
Before we can smile at each other,
    we must learn to look at each other.

53
THE MOON ABOVE, THE EARTH BELOW
Fifteenth Sunday of the Year (C)

- Deuteronomy 30:10–14
- Colossians 1:15–20
- Luke 10:25–37

On Thursday of this week
    we will celebrate the twentieth anniversary
    of the Eagle's landing on the moon.
We will hear over and over on the media
    those thrilling words of Neil Armstrong,
        "That's one small step for man, one giant leap for mankind."
The other night,
    CBS documented the historic landing on the moon
    with a special entitled, "The Moon Above, the Earth Below."
The title described the mingling of two worlds.
While we witnessed our dramatic first flight to the moon,
    we also heard Charles Kuralt narrate old clips
    of what Americans were doing back on earth on July 20, 1969.
There were clips from weddings, hospitals,
    and factories where workers sewed the astronauts' suits.
We listened to people at the supper table
    and at the neighborhood bar.
The program was the clashing of two worlds,
    one heavenly and one mundane.

Have you ever stopped to ask yourself
    why you come to mass on Sunday?
Why do we leave our mundane world
    and come into a heavenly world each week?

229

I've been reading a book this week called *The Emerging Parish.*[1]
It's a sociological study of American Catholic life
   since Vatican II.
In one of the surveys,
   Catholics were asked why they attended Sunday mass.
I was happy to note that only six percent said they came to mass
   because the church required it.
The survey claimed that thirty-seven percent said that they
     "enjoyed the feeling of meditating and communicating with God."
It also noted that twenty percent said
   that they "felt a need to receive the sacrament of holy communion,"
   and nineteen percent felt that they "need to hear God's word."
In other words, most Catholics come to mass
   because they want to feel close to God.

It's been said that statistics don't lie
   but interpreters do.
Just how do we truthfully interpret these statistics that tell us
   that most Catholics come to mass to feel close to God?
For example, do we come to church on Sunday
   "to fill up on God,"
   something like filling up our spiritual tanks
   to get us through the rest of the week?
Do we come to escape the absurdity of our daily world
   to find a heavenly world with our own tranquility base?

When the first Soviet cosmonauts came back to earth
   they declared that they hadn't seen God in the heavens.
A silly commentary.
But there is a sense in which they were correct.
Often, even religious people have a static view of God:
   God is in another world,
   up there!
And only by very special means

---

[1] Joseph Gremillion and Jim Castelli, *The Emerging Parish: The Notre Dame Study of Catholic Life Since Vatican II* (San Francisco: Harper & Row, 1987) pp. 134–135.

can we ever come close to God.
For some, God is only found in the Bible,
    or in the eucharist,
    or in some secret formula for which you have to bargain.

Two believers struggle with the question
    of God's place in our world
    in today's scriptures.
The first is Moses who, in his farewell sermon,
    tells his people not to look for the meaning of God
    in something mysterious and remote.
God's commandments are no longer written on tablets of stone,
    but are engraved on the heart.
God's law "is something very near to you,
    already in your mouths and in your hearts;
    you have only to carry it out."

The second believer is a lawyer.
He believes in God and knows his catechism.
He knows that the law says to love God and neighbor as yourself.
But the business of lawyers is precision.
They must always be sure of definitions.
And so, he asks,
    "Who is my neighbor?"

No matter how we try,
    we can never get the full shock of Jesus' answer.
His parable of the good Samaritan
    blew the sandals off his listeners' feet.
For the Jews, Samaritans were radically impure,
    politically dangerous
    and religiously heretical.
For generations the Jews had been told,
    even by their great prophets
    like Hosea and Ezekiel,
    that the Samaritans were definitely not neighbors.

The priest and the levite pass by the man in the ditch.
It's easy to stereotype these two religious leaders.
I remember, in the play "Godspell,"
    how prim and proper they came across.
One of the purposes of a play is to contrast

the good guys with the bad guys.
But life is more complicated than that.
The priest and the levite probably were moved by the pitiful victim.
No doubt they stopped to look
   and they almost became
   the good priest and the good levite.
But something kept them from doing the human thing:
   the law.
The story says that the man was "half-dead."
The priest and the levite,
   despite their feelings of pity,
   were bound by the law
   which said they would be ritually impure
   if they touched a corpse.
The law won out over the law engraved on their hearts.
Heaven clashed with earth
   and heaven won.

The Samaritan is "moved to pity at the sight."
He proves to be neighbor because he acts like a neighbor.
The Samaritan's heavenly world,
   his religious world,
   pays attention to his daily world.
His God is not in the sky
   but very near.
I think the story of the good Samaritan
   gives us insight into our question
   of why we come to mass on Sunday.
The desire to feel closer to God
   is one of the most human desires of our hearts.
But the true goal of our Sunday worship
   in word and sacrament
   is to make us aware
   that God is not just in church
   but in our lives.
God's grace is not locked up in a church building
   or in a Bible or a tabernacle or a homily.
God's grace is in the world,
   especially in those times and events
   when we seem empty or at our wits' end,
   when our journey to Jericho is interrupted by strange demands.

We come to church on Sunday as a believing community
   not to "get God,"
   but to celebrate a world of grace
   and a God who is very near.

54
THE BETTER PART
Sixteenth Sunday of the Year (C)

- Genesis 18:1–10
- Colossians 1:24–28
- Luke 10:38–42

We were bombarded this past week with
   clips of the Eagle landing on the moon.
Bombarded also were the three aging astronauts.
News reporters asked Neil Armstrong, Edwin Aldrin and Mike Collins
   the same "in depth" questions over and over again,
   like, "How did landing on the moon
   affect your personal lives?"
At times they sounded not like scientists but poets
   when they talked about looking up at the sky
   on a summer's eve from a backyard barbecue
   and wondering about their tiny footprints on the moon.

Aldrin spoke not just about how his life had changed on the moon
   but of the dramatic changes that took place in his personal life
   when he came back to earth.
I've always been fascinated with the character of Edwin Aldrin.
With a name like Edwin,
   he probably had to fight every inch of his life.
Maybe that's why he preferred to be called "Buzz";
   it sounds more macho and more appropriate for an astronaut.
But even with the name "Buzz,"
   he missed the historic achievement
   of becoming the first man on the moon
   by one shy guy named Neil.
Aldrin will go down in history with the bitter-sweet tag:
   "The *second* man to set foot on the moon."

Buzz Aldrin is writing his autobiography.
Like his tag, his story will also be bitter-sweet.
He'll write about the rigidly structured training program before Apollo.
It was an ordered training, centered entirely outside himself.
When Buzz returned to earth
   to face the significant people of his life,
   all orderliness and programmed expectations suddenly vanished.
Despite his costly and elaborate training,
   he had never developed the inner resources and center needed
   to cope with his life and his times.
Indeed, he was chosen to go to the moon in the first place
   because he appeared to be a well-ordered cog
   in the space machine.
But when he faced the ordinary challenges
   of his personal and family life,
   he collapsed and had, in his words,
   "a good old-fashioned American nervous breakdown."
His book will describe his bouts with booze,
   depression, self doubt
   and the eventual recovery and centering of his life.

Jesus' close friend Martha could sympathize with Buzz Aldrin.
She too was burdened with her name.
Martha meant "lady" or "mistress" of a household.
She felt, therefore, that she had to act like the "lady of the house"
   and do what proper ladies had always done,
   at least since the time of Sarah:
   sweat it out in the kitchen
   and make a tasty meal for the men.

Like Aldrin, Martha knew what it meant to come in second place.
That didn't seem to be the case at first.
After all, Martha was the one who stuck her neck out
   to welcome the fugitive Jesus into the house.
Martha is the one who took down
   The Joy of Cooking from the pantry shelf.
Luke says she busied herself
   "with all the details of hospitality."
She did what was expected of the "lady of the house,"
   and she did it well.
She acted exactly like the good Samaritan
   whom Jesus praised last week.

But when it came to first place,
  that honor went to the shy, quiet one, Mary.
Mary took a revolutionary step for a woman
  and sat at a rabbi's feet
  and listened to his teaching.

Sadly, down through history,
  preachers have assured Martha's second place.
Martha represented the Christian apostolate of activism,
  while Mary represented the contemplative vocation;
  the active apostolate was good,
  but the contemplative vocation was number one.

But that interpretation reads too much into the story.
The story of Martha and Mary is a living parable.
It was intended to show a contrast
  between those who believed they could be saved
  by works according to the law,
  and those who believed they could be saved
  by the word of Jesus.
Jesus doesn't put Martha in second place.
After all, a meal had to be prepared and guests had to be served.
Jesus tells her that her real problem
  is that she is overly anxious about secondary matters.
He invites her not to abandon her work but to center her life.

The twentieth anniversary of Eagle's landing on the moon
  reminds us of the wondrous gifts and blessings of
  our technological world.
Our scientists ask "How can we do it better?"
  and they do it.
But there are also other questions that need to be asked.
They are the questions asked by poets, artists, preachers,
  who ponder, with the community,
  the living word of God.
  questions like:
    Why are we putting our work before our families?
    Why are we putting our false egos before our love and our service?
    Why are we putting our house before our home?
    Why are we putting our nation before humankind?
    Why are we putting our dominance and pleasure before
      our precious environment?

Why are we fretting over secondary things when only one thing is
    necessary?

Buzz Aldrin's parable tells us the down side
    of our technological age.
We can get so wrapped up in a noisy, demanding, impersonal world
    that we forget who we are.
We can lose perspective,
    a center,
    a way of "seeing in the dark."

Maybe the most revolutionary,
    the most freeing thing we can do is pray.
It's not easy to find time to pray these days.
How can a young mother of three kids find time to pray?
How do you pray in a van pool on the way to work?
In an age that places such a priority on efficiency,
    prayer isn't very cost-effective.
We must learn to pray
    not to be relieved from our demanding world,
    but to center our lives in the midst of this world.
None of us can run from the responsibilities
    of the Martha in our lives.
But none of us can afford to ignore the freedom
    of the Mary in our lives.

55
MORE THAN MISTAKES HAVE BEEN MADE
Twenty-First Sunday of the Year (C)

- Isaiah 66:18–21
- Hebrews 12:5–7,11–13
- Luke 13:22–30

About once a month I answer the doorbell
    to a pair of God's hucksters.
Eager-looking Jehovah's Witnesses or well-scrubbed Mormons try
    to convince me
    that only a few in number will be saved
    and that their church represents those blessed few.

Unfortunately, for them, they don't have a clue
    as to who it is who answers the door.
At first I used to relish these uninvited visits.
I enjoyed confronting their smugness
    with all the biblical, historical, and theological ammunition
    I could muster.
Of course, nothing was accomplished
    in these battles at the doorstep.
They walked away with smug determination.
I closed my door with smug satisfaction.
Maybe I've begun to mellow,
    but recently I simply tell God's peddlers,
    "Thank you and have a nice day."

The person who tapped Jesus on the shoulder in today's gospel was
    also smug:
        "Lord, are they few in number who are to be saved?"
He represents those in our Lord's time

who believed they were saved
    simply because they belonged to the "in" group.
Jesus refuses to get caught up in such a silly argument.
He doesn't even give a straight answer.
Instead, he throws them a curve ball,
    "Try to come in through the narrow door. . . .
    Some who are last will be first,
    and some who are first will be last."

When Luke wrote this gospel,
    Jerusalem and the temple had already been destroyed.
But Luke wasn't telling his listeners
    that the smug fellow in the story
    represented just those who refused to accept the Messiah.
The "you" of Jesus' answer is not singular but plural.
In other words, Jesus is speaking
    to the Christians of Luke's time as well.
He's telling them,
    "Just because you are a Christian,
    part of the 'in' group,
    doesn't mean you should gloat
    over what happened to Jerusalem."
Jesus tells them not to rest on their laurels
    and act so smugly.

Smugness is an evil not just reserved
    to creepy characters in the Bible
    nor to today's polyester prophets.
Smugness abounds in the so-called "heroes" of our day.
It seems that whenever big stars, politicians, TV preachers,
    are caught in the act of a crime,
    they seem to show more concern for legal technicalities
    than for ethical principles.
The most they are willing to admit is,
    "Mistakes were made"—
    loosely translated, "I was caught."

It seems so difficult for the heroes and heroines of our time
    to break from smugness
    and to apologize for their sins.
More than a week after the Valdez disaster,
    L.G. Rawls, the chairman of Exxon, finally apologized.

Well, sort of.
Rawls declared,
   "I want to tell you how sorry I am
   that this accident took place."
Note in that hollow sentence
   no ownership of responsibility.
Why couldn't he apologize to the people
   and the animals of Alaska?

What has caused this modern smugness to descend upon our land?
What makes our heroes think they are above the law
   and do not owe us an apology?
What makes them think that they belong
   to some privileged "in group"
   with its own rules of conduct?
Did it begin with the schmaltzy novel *Love Story*
   where Oliver is told,
      "Love means never having to say you're sorry"?
Did it begin when Richard Nixon claimed,
   "I am not a crook"
   and substituted "Mea culpa, mea culpa"
   with the now popular line,
   "Mistakes were made"?
Is it the result of the 700,000 lawyers in America?
That's one for every 350 citizens.
Their first bit of advice in law suits
   is never to admit you are wrong.

Or does the problem of smugness in our land stem from
   something deeper?
Have we lost one of the key insights of our biblical tradition:
   that we, whether members of the "in" group or the "out" group,
   are all capable of evil
   and are also free to choose to do good?

Conservatives preach as if there are only two kinds of people in society:
   "the criminals" destined to commit evil acts,
   and the rest of us,
   who are by nature, more or less, rather good people.
Such a simplistic painting of the world
   in shades of black and white,
      prevents conservatives from ever owning up

to the shadow side of their lives
and ever discovering the good Samaritans
and the prodigal sons and daughters
of our time.

Liberals, on the other hand,
    are so bent on blaming society and environment
    for all the violence and ugliness of our times
    that they fail to recognize the individual capacity each of us has
    to choose evil or to choose good.
The truly wise of this earth
    are skeptical of liberal sentimentalism.
They know that love means you *have* to say you're sorry
    until your dying day.

The gospel today reminds us
    that we religious people, in particular,
    can succumb to the sin of smugness
    as we battle those "not saved."
We should remember the story of St. Anthony
    who went out into the desert
    to fight the devil.
At the end of his life of battle,
    he taught that we must learn to find good,
    even in the devil.

We eat and drink today in the company of Jesus
    who banishes our smugness
    and opens up for us
    a narrow door.

56
EXAMINE YOUR EYES
AND CHECK UNDER YOUR NOSE
Twenty-Second Sunday of the Year (C)

- Sirach 3:17–18,20,28–29
- Hebrews 12:18–19,22–24
- Luke 14:1,7–14

On Friday I did something I haven't done for about eight years:
    I had an eye examination.
The optometrist chided me for waiting so long.
"Every two or three years should be the rule," he warned.
Through his sophisticated lenses,
    the doctor could tell that I had mowed my lawn before coming to
    his office;
    he saw a tiny bit of grass in my eye.
This observation led him to ask,
    "How's the weather out there today?
    You know, I'm in this office from 9 to 6 each day.
    Since there are no windows here,
    I never know if the sun is shining or not."
What a sense of irony!
The doctor who could observe the tiny bit of grass in my eye
    had no window to see the last sunny days of summer.

So much of the gospel is about the irony of seeing
    what others fail to see.
Our gospel story today begins with the note
    that when Jesus walked into the dining room,
    "they observed him closely."
The word used for "observe" indicates that the Pharisees
    were watching Jesus with a sinister intent.
There was good reason for the Pharisees
    to observe Jesus so closely.

He already had a reputation for ignoring
   the dinner rules of Miss Manners.
There had been those two previous meals
   where he shocked the guests.
There was that meal where he allowed a sinner
   to perfume his feet.
There was also the meal where he began eating
   without ceremoniously washing his hands.
And now there was this meal at a leading Pharisee's house,
   which was not just an ordinary meal
   but a sabbath dinner.
They wondered what new act of bad manners
   the rabbi from Nazareth
   would commit at this sacred meal.
That's why "they observed him closely."

It's sad that the next five verses
   have been sliced out of today's gospel.
Immediately after the phrase "they observed him closely," we read that
   "Directly in front of him
   was a man who suffered from dropsy" (Luke 14:2).
Jesus once again broke all the rules
   by healing the man on the sabbath.
There is a thread of irony that runs throughout
   this dinner story.
The Pharisees weren't the only ones
   who were observing things closely.
Jesus, too, had his eyes wide open.
He noticed the suffering man in front of him
   and healed him immediately.
Of course, the man with dropsy was also in front of the Pharisees.
So why is it that they overlooked him?
Was it because they were too sinister
   in their observation of Jesus?
Was it because they were too busy scrambling
   to get a good seat at the head table?
Whatever the reason,
   their religious flaw seems to be
   that they were looking in the wrong place.

And because they looked in the wrong place,
   they not only failed to see the suffering man in front of them,
   but also failed to recognize that Jesus, the guest,

was really the host,
inviting all to God's eternal banquet.

Years ago, the Baptist theologian, Harvey Cox, wrote that
"If God reads *Time* magazine,
he doesn't first read the section on 'Religion,'
but reads the section on the 'World'
which is the stage of his activity."
It was Cox's way of reminding us
not to look for God in the wrong place.
I have tried to remember that advice
but must confess that I sometimes fall into temptation on
Saturday mornings.
That's the day when the Washington *Post*
has a section on "Religion,"
usually found somewhere between the sections on
"Style" and "Sports."

Lately I've begun to observe a certain motif
in the "Religion" section.
So many of the articles are about
the various churches of our time
struggling to deal with persons
long overlooked by religious people:
Polish Catholics throwing water on Jewish protesters at Auschwitz;
mainline Protestant denominations voting to either reject or accept
women for ordination,
or whether to allow homosexuals and lesbians into
their congregations;
American bishops writing long documents on why only ordained men
can preach;
Vatican officials upset that so many American Catholics are granted
annulments;
blacks and Hispanics demanding full status in
the Christian community;
religious leaders gathering to decide how to respond to people with
AIDS, to leaders of NOW, to the oppressed of South Africa.

After two thousand years,
the church is still struggling to embrace the vulnerable,
the poor, the "unclean," the "sinner"
in our midst.

But something new is happening in our time.
The church no longer has the capacity nor the luxury
   to ignore those who for so long have been overlooked.
They are standing in front of us and they will not go away.
They are demanding we see them and hear them and welcome them
   as sisters and brothers.

The gospel today reminds us
   that Jesus not only had a big heart but big eyes.
Before we can learn to love like him,
   we must learn to see like him
   those who are in front of us.

57

SIGNS OF MUSTARD SEED FAITH
Twenty-Seventh Sunday of the Year (C)

- Habakkuk 1:2–3; 2:2–4
- 2 Timothy 1:6–8,13–14
- Luke 17:5–10

(The social justice committee of the parish planned the liturgy of this particular Sunday. A clothes tree stood in the sanctuary. During the opening hymn, leaders of social justice groups in the parish carried various symbols of their ministries. Each placed a symbol on the clothes tree before the mass began.)

Each semester I hear in preaching class
   at least four homilies about Mother Teresa.
Now I can understand why my students choose to elevate this
   holy woman,
      whose mission to the "poorest of the poor"
   has captured the imagination and respect of the world community.
Mother Teresa has been given a secular canonization
   with her Nobel Peace prize.
Even unbelievers behold this frail nun as a saint.
But I often wonder if preachers unwittingly give the impression
   that only saints are called to works of justice and love,
   and that saints are rare and religiously clad,
      living in far-off places like Calcutta.

While I appreciate the homiletic stories of Mother Teresa,
   once in a while I wish we could hear some stories of faith
   about less known saints.
When you read the gospels,
   you will seldom find Jesus pointing to the obvious saints,
   but to those whom others failed to see:

the centurion,
the tax collector,
a woman of the streets.

Yesterday in DC, in a march for the plight of our homeless,
    one could spot such a woman of faith:
    actress Susan Sarandon.
This sultry actress would probably be amazed
    that I singled her out as a "woman of faith."
Certainly her former teachers at Catholic University's
    Drama Department would be amazed.
After all, hasn't her personal life come awfully close
    to the loose women she has portrayed on the silver screen?
She's definitely not the Mother Teresa type,
    and yet somehow she has never forgotten the Catholic tradition
    of commitment to social justice and love
    that she learned at the university.

When a reporter asked her the other day
    why she picked such social concerns as AIDS ministry and
    the homeless,
    Ms. Sarandon said,
        "How could someone not notice the plight of these people?
        Living in New York, I see it every day.
        I didn't pick these people nor these issues;
        they picked me!"

Susan Sarandon may never win the Nobel Peace Prize
    and probably won't be canonized.
But somehow I think she would be just the kind of person of faith
    that Jesus would point to in his Sunday homily today.
She doesn't wait for some press agent
    to choose her "favorite charity"
    nor ask for an "increase of faith"
    so that she can move sycamores.
She simply does the best she can
    with her mustard seed faith.

Mustard seed faith is what Jesus talked about
    when the apostles asked him to increase their faith.
Jesus tells them that it is not a question of more or less faith,
    but how you live with the little faith you've got left.

It is not a question of marveling at what great saints can do,
 but what we all can do
 for those in need of justice and love.
Many of our sisters and brothers in the world today
 join the lament of the prophet Habakkuk and cry out,
  "How long, O Lord?
  I cry out for help but you do not listen!"
We Catholic Christians have not picked
 the victims of poverty, racism, sexism, the homeless and
 the disheartened;
 they have picked us
 and are crying out not just to the Lord,
 but to us.

The social concerns of today can so overwhelm us
 that we, too, can be tempted to run away from our gospel duty.
The problems are as big and as deeply rooted
 as the sycamore tree.
What can one person do?
What can one person with a little mustard seed faith
 possibly do to make a difference?
Don't I have to be a saint with great faith to make a dent?

One of the saints of our time
 was Dorothy Day of New York's Catholic Worker.
Her hair in a bun,
 her clothes left over from a clothing drive,
 Dorothy Day fed and housed the poor
 with the kind of no-fuss manner
 of the servant in today's gospel parable.
She hated when people would call her "a saint."
She saw it as a cop-out:
 "Don't say that.
 Don't make it too easy for yourself.
 You say that to convince yourself
 that you are different from me,
 that I am different from you.
 I am not different from you.
 I am not a saint.
 I am like you.
 You could easily do what I do.
 You don't need any more than what you have."

We look not just to the sycamore tree,
   but to the clothes tree
   that stands in our sanctuary today.
It's a simple reminder of what many saints
   in this community of Good Shepherd
   are already doing with their mustard seed faith.

On the clothes tree are various signs
   of the social justice ministries of our parish.
The Crop Walk Sign reminds us
   of those who will walk on October 21
   for donations which will aid our local community needs.
The carpenter's apron is a sign
   of the Good Shepherd Housing Project
   that tackles such tough issues as affordable housing
   for nurses, teachers and policemen and women in Fairfax County.
The basket of food, the poor box, the winter coat
   are signs of such ministries as S.O.M.E.,
   the United Community Ministries
   and the ministries of our students who will receive
   the sacrament of confirmation this Friday
   after completing fifteen hours of community service.
The boxes of books below the clothes tree remind us
   of the many hours of service given by our parishioners in
   tutoring prisoners.

These signs of mustard seed faith in our own community
   remind us of our common call to Christian service.
These signs of mustard seed faith can turn the phrase
   "It can't be done" to
   "It is already being done."

58
ARE ALL RELIGIOUS PEOPLE PHONY?
Thirtieth Sunday of the Year (C)

- Sirach 35:12–14
- 2 Timothy 4:6–8,16–18
- Luke 18:9–14

Last Wednesday in Charlotte, North Carolina,
    Judge Robert Potter was not impressed with Jim Bakker
    when he told the judge,
    "I have sinned. I've made mistakes."
Judge Potter lived up to his nickname, "Maximum Bob,"
    by sentencing Bakker to forty-five years in prison
    and a half million dollar fine.
In handing down the sentence, Judge Potter said,
    "Those of us who do have religion
    are sick of being saps for money-grubbing preachers and priests."

Priests?
Did he say priests?
When "Maximum Bob" spoke these stinging words,
    Father Bob wondered why the judge included priests
    in his condemnation of religious phonies.
After all, wasn't it only fundamentalist TV evangelists
    who were giving a bad name to religion?
Why priests?

Have we entered an age where there are no sacred cows?
Has the media crossed over the line in exposing the dirty linen
    not just of movie stars and politicians
    but of religious leaders as well?
Geraldo, Sally Jessie, Phil and Oprah

have all told us
what priests, nuns, and ministers are really like!
We have more than just clay feet;
  we have greedy hands and hearts as well.

Now don't get me wrong.
I don't suggest that we return to the days
  when religious leaders were put so high on pedestals
  that we forgot they were human.
I remember those days
  when kids in Catholic schools were shocked
  to find out that nuns went to the bathroom.
I'm not hinting at a return to those good old days
  when Father *always* knew best
  and the rest of the parish knew nothing.

What I am wondering about is this new scape-goating
  where we can easily point to the phoniness
  of our religious leaders
  to get ourselves off the hook.

It's a good thing that "Maximum Bob" wasn't in the temple
  the day the Pharisee went up there to pray.
He never would have had a chance.
He would have pointed out what preachers have done for centuries:
  how all Pharisees were phonies;
  how the Pharisee was in the front of the temple
  praying not to God,
  but to himself;
  how real religious people stay
  in the back of the temple
  beating their breasts
  and centering only on their sins.

If "Maximum Bob" did make these judgments,
  Father Bob would say,
      "Now wait just a minute!
    Let's go back to the temple
    and see and hear what really happened that day."
You can be sure that there were more than two men at prayer in
  the temple.

The place was filled with devout Jews
   since it was the custom to go to the temple three times a day to pray:
   9 A.M., noon, and 3 P.M.
It's easy to pick on this one Pharisee
   who prayed like little Jack Horner,
      "What a good boy am I!"
But that doesn't mean that all the Pharisees
   were praying that way.
The temple was filled with other Pharisees
   who prayed not to themselves,
   but honestly to God.

Religious people don't have exclusive rights to phoniness.
And why do we assume that the Pharisee prayed in the *front*
   while the tax collector prayed in the *back* of the temple?
The only thing Luke says in the parable
   is that the tax collector
   "kept his distance."
He couldn't have been that far away from the Pharisee who noticed him
   when he thanked God that he wasn't like "this tax collector."
When we miss this point,
   we continue the tradition of back-pew Catholics,
   who, in an ironic way, think they are less phony
   than the folks up front.
There is an old Irish saying that captures this myth nicely:
   "Never trust anybody in the front pew!"
But if we make that judgment,
   we miss the heart of this parable.
We all stand in need of God because all of us,
   those up front and those in the back,
   those wearing miters and those wearing baseball caps,
   to some extent have been phony in our dealings with one another.

We are complex.
Walt Whitman said it best:
   "I am large; I contain a multitude."
There is saint and sinner in each of us.
And that's the person Jesus is calling us to recognize.
He is not telling us to beat our breasts
   and dwell only on our phoniness.
He is not telling us to judge all religous people as phonies.
He is calling all of us to stand before God in honesty.

Years ago, when I was studying speech communication
   in graduate school,
   I came across an M.A. thesis analyzing the prayers
   that were prayed by the famous Chaplain Peter Marshall
   at the beginning of congressional sessions.
One of the first steps in rhetorical criticism is to ask:
   Who is the audience of the speech?
I found it amusing that the student who wrote this particular thesis
   had a difficult time determining who was the audience of
   Dr. Marshall's prayers:
      God or Congress?

The gospels tell us that Jesus never found it difficult
   to determine who his audience was when he prayed.
In the temple,
   on the road,
   even on the cross,
   he prayed honestly to God.
The prayer of Jesus reminds us that
   since God knows no favorites,
   there's no reason to fake it.

FEASTS

59
LET'S MAKE EVERYONE
A EUCHARISTIC MINISTER
Corpus Christi (The Body of Christ) (A)

- Deuteronomy 8:2–3,14–16
- 1 Corinthians 10:16–17
- John 6:51–58

(While a homilist should not feel compelled to preach a "Father's Day homily," a homilist should also not dismiss the creative possibilities of making connections between two seemingly different images.)

Of course, there is no direct connection between today's
   Feast of Corpus Christi and Father's Day.
But there is a sense in which the image of a father
   is a good place to begin our reflection
   on the body of Christ.
Mothers are thrilled to hold their babies for the first time.
But the child that the mother holds is the tiny body
   that she has grown to know inside of her for nine months.
It's a gradual process of recognition.
With a father, it's different.
When a father first sees his newborn child
   it's a miraculous, sudden introduction.[1]

I remember over thirty years ago
   rushing with my brother Frank to a hospital nursery
   to see his newborn son.

---

[1] I owe this insight to Frederick Buechner, *Whistling in the Dark: An ABC Theologized* (San Francisco: Harper & Row, 1988) p. 47.

As we pressed our faces against the glass window,
   we read the lips of the nurse
   who held little Frankie in her arms:
      "Yes, Mr. Waznak, he's *your son.*"
I've never seen my brother's eyes
   so filled with wonder and delight.
He was awe-struck by the sight of this bundle of his body.

There was a time when Christians looked upon the eucharist
   as fathers looked upon their newborn children—
   they were in awe at the sight of the body.
This Feast of the Body of Christ dates to the thirteenth century
   when for many historical reasons
   believers went from altar to altar
   to look at the consecrated host.
Many expected favors and answers to prayers
   by participating in this private devotion.
These believers became so wrapped up in gazing on the body of Christ
   that they stopped receiving the body of Christ.

At the beginning of our century
   the practice of frequent communion
   was reintroduced into our church.
Then came the reforms of the Second Vatican Council
   that invited us not just to look at the body of Christ,
   but to receive and become the body of Christ.
Just as a father soon learns that his role
   is not just to gaze on his child
   but to nurture and communicate with the child,
   so, too, we as a church were taught to do the same with the eucharist.
We came to realize that the eucharist was not just a devotion
   where we entered into a private communication with Jesus,
   but a time to receive and become the body of Christ.

This new emphasis on the eucharist continues in our own day.
Just three years ago, Pope John Paul II wrote in an encyclical:
   "All of us who take part in the eucharist
   are called to discover, through this sacrament,
   the profound meaning of our actions in the world
   in favor of development and peace,
   and to receive from it the strength to commit ourselves
   ever more generously,

following the example of Christ
who in this sacrament lays down his life for his friends."[2]
The pope reminded us
　　that it is not enough to gaze upon the body of Christ,
　　not enough to receive the body of Christ.
We are invited to become the body of Christ.

There's always something more to discover
　　about the food that God gives to us.
That is what our scriptures for this Feast of Corpus Christi tell us today.
Moses reminded the people
　　that the manna that sustained them in their desert journey
　　was more than sweet juice from desert shrubs;
　　manna was God's food for God's people,
　　manna was God's fulfillment of a promise to be
　　not only *with* them
　　but *for* them
　　through their journey in the desert.

In today's gospel Jesus told the people something new
　　about the food that God gave them.
As wonderful and heavenly as the manna in the desert was,
　　he was the new manna,
　　God's final food.
When they received his body and blood,
　　they shared God's own life.

The Christians in St. Paul's day were receiving the body of Christ,
　　but not becoming the body of Christ.
The church in Corinth had great liturgies
　　but was a scandalous community
　　because the rich did not share with the poor
　　and the strong did not reach out to the weak.
St. Paul encouraged the Corinthian church not just to receive
　　the body of Christ
　　but to become the body of Christ.

---

[2] Pope John Paul II, *Sollicitudo Rei Socialis,* 98:5.

The Feast of Corpus Christi invites us
  to discover something more about the food that God gives us.
We now have eucharistic ministers at our liturgies
  whose privilege it is to distribute the body of Christ.
Over and over again,
  they announce to those who approach God's table:
  "The body of Christ."
Eucharistic ministers gradually come to realize that when they say
    these words
  they are not just giving the body of Christ,
  but they are becoming the body of Christ.
In bringing the body of Christ to the sick and the elderly
  eucharistic ministers become more like Christ
  in the sharing of their lives.

I wish that we could begin a new tradition in our church
  where every member of the parish would be designated
  a eucharistic minister,
  where people of all ages and colors and levels of faith
  could take turns each Sunday
  in this service to God's people.
If this were to happen,
  all of you would begin to appreciate the thrill
  of not only giving the body of Christ,
  but seeing in a new way the people who approach the altar
  as the body of Christ.
In bringing the body of Christ to the community,
  you would begin to think less of yourself
  and more of others.
If such a day would come,
  maybe we would become more of a church of the real presence:
    a church not just receiving the body of Christ,
    but becoming the body of Christ.
It would give a whole new meaning to the word "communion."

60
KING FROM A CROSS
Feast of Christ the King (C)

- 2 Samuel 5:1–3
- Colossians 1:12–20
- Luke 23:35–43

On his ninetieth birthday,
    Oliver Wendell Holmes, Jr. was asked by a reporter,
    "What has been the secret of your success?"
The illustrious justice solemnly responded:
    "Young man, the secret of my success
    is that at an early age
    I discovered that I was not God."

History would have been eminently more peaceful and productive
    if only its rulers would have discovered the same lesson:
    that they were not God.
Throughout history, rulers were considered divine
    because like God they too held the power of life and death over
    their subjects.
Rome's emperors proclaimed that indeed they were living gods,
Europe's kings and queens lorded over their subjects
    because of their "divine right."
It wasn't until the end of World War II
    that the people of Japan could gaze upon their emperor Hirohito
    not as a god
    but as a man.

Earlier in this century,
    Pope Pius XI realized that Europe's royal kingdoms
    would soon become the stuff of fairy tales.
But the pope was convinced that the new rulers of such kingdoms

as nazism, socialism and communism
eventually would not save people
because these modern kingdoms would also lord it over their subjects
and rob them of their freedom as daughters and sons of God.
Pius XI wanted to challenge these new emerging kingdoms.
He wanted to lead people to the one true throne.
And so he proclaimed this Feast of Christ the King.

Because the Feast of Christ the King emerged
   from such a particular political scene,
   it isn't always a relevant feast to celebrate.
After all, we are Americans,
   living in a democratic republic.
The metaphor of king seems foreign to us.

And so what happens is that we often end up with
   a hodgepodge celebration:
      preaching how Christ is king of our hearts
      on a feast which is supposed to celebrate his kingship
      not over our individual hearts,
      but over the universe.
On this feast, some celebrants wear gold vestments
   and choirs blast out triumphant hymns—
   all that on a feast about a king who dies naked on a cross between
   two criminals.

But this year, the Feast of Christ the King, 1989, is different.
Europe was shaking in its boots
   when this feast was first celebrated.
In these past weeks we have watched Europe dance in its boots
   with a new burst of energy and liberation:
      a non-communist prime minister rules Poland;
      at the beginning of winter, a new Prague spring returns to
         Czechoslovakia;
      East and West Germans deliriously dance on the wall that once
         divided them.
This year, 1989, the Feast of Christ the King takes on new meaning.
What is most remarkable about the new reforms sweeping
   Eastern Europe
   is that so far, thank God,
   it has been a bloodless revolution.
It's as if ordinary citizens

suddenly have come to realize their God-given rights
  and to believe in their ability to move kings and "isms"
  by a voice of human solidarity.
Suddenly, without tanks or guns,
  but with a loud voice of protest,
  they have told their rulers,
    "You are not God."

We surrender our souls whenever we fail to speak to our rulers,
  be they communists or congresspersons,
  parents or teachers,
  bosses or pastors.
We surrender our souls whenever we remain silent
  when those who rule over us
  forget that they are not God.

The reason why we proclaim Christ as our king
  is that he taught us what real leadership is all about.
The reason why he reigns from a cross
  is that he never failed to remind the political and religious rulers
  of his time
  that they weren't gods.
Christ is a king who is still listening to his subjects
  and taking their words to heart
  even as he dies on a cross.
He listens even to the angry and selfish criminal to his left.
And he listens to the hopeful criminal whom legend calls Dismas.
He assures him,
    "This day you will be with me in paradise."

And Christ the king still listens to us as we pray this day:
"We proclaim you as our king, Christ our Lord.
We pray for the wisdom and the courage always to speak your
  gospel truth,
  especially to those who have power over our lives.
We pray too for the gift of patience
  to listen to those people who depend upon us
  for leadership and purpose.
Help Presidents Bush and Gorbachev
  in their meeting in Malta.
Give them the courage to make right and just decisions.
Help them not to fear the boldness of leadership.

Bless the people of Eastern Europe
   and help them choose leaders
   who will serve them wisely.
Give strength to the people all over our globe
   who are striving for human rights and dignity,
   like the people in China, South Africa, Lebanon,
   whose walls of shame still stand.
May the shepherds of your church
   continue to speak out against violence and social injustice;
   and may they also learn to listen
   to the cries and concerns of the people.
We thank you for ending this last Sunday of the church year
   on such a note of hope.
In all things,
   and in our own day,
   Christ our King,
   may your kingdom come
   and may your will be done. Amen."

61
MARY'S ROLE
Feast of the Assumption of Mary

- Revelation 11:19; 12:1–6,10
- 1 Corinthians 15:20–26
- Luke 1:39–56

Women in our day sit in Congress
    and the cockpits of jet airliners.
They take their place as co-partners
    in the work force of our nation.
But there are still some places
    where women cannot achieve their rightful role.
Oddly, one of these places is in the movies.
Actresses complain that the good roles
    are still written for men.
Only occasionally does a film come along
    where women are given prominent roles.

And while women do have prominent roles throughout the Bible,
    it's rare that we hear them talking to one another.
Today's Feast of the Assumption features a rare treat:
    two women in conversation,
    a significant conversation.
Luke decides to place this conversation
    between Mary and Elizabeth
    right at the beginning of his story of Jesus.
Luke seems to be telling us that in this conversation
    between the two mothers-to-be
    lies the key to what Jesus will do for us
    in the history of salvation.

265

The song that Mary sings, her Magnificat,
    tells us that the salvation that the Messiah will bring
    is not just for special people.
Indeed, God has a peculiar affection for ordinary people,
    for the lowly,
    the servants,
    the confused,
    the hungry,
    people as ordinary as a pregnant young girl
    on a hasty visit to her old pregnant cousin.

To understand and appreciate this Feast of the Assumption,
    indeed to understand and appreciate the role of Mary
    in our Christian tradition,
    is to realize that there were times in history
    when the ordinary, lowly servant of God, Mary,
    captured a most important role.

Those were the times
    when, for various reasons,
    the divinity of Jesus was emphasized over his humanity.
This made the resurrection something distant,
    something seemingly impossible for the ordinary Christian.
And so we turned to Mary.

Her role in salvation, however,
    was something done by God
    for one like us,
    ordinary humans.
We looked to the tender,
    lowly Mary of Nazareth,
    for the possibility that we, too,
    would one day be risen in Christ.

In our present time
    we have grown closer to the humanity of Jesus
    as well as to his divinity.
It's not surprising, then,
    that in such times,
    when Jesus is more accessible to us,
    Mary takes on a different role for some people.

Some modern images of Mary picture her
   not as the lowly, human servant,
   but as a stern judge of the world,
   warning us of all sorts of disasters
   if we don't follow "her" advice.

It's important, therefore, that we keep intact
   the biblical role of Mary
   that we hear proclaimed in our gospel today.
There is hope here in the ordinary young woman of Nazareth.
There is hope for us in this role of Mary,
   who despite all odds
   continues to believe that God will do great things for us.

What God has done for Mary,
   he will do for us,
   if, like her,
   we will believe in God's promises.

62
JUST SAY YES
Feast of the Immaculate Conception

- Genesis 3:9–15,20
- Ephesians 1:3–6,11–12
- Luke 1:26–38

The media hinted that Mikhail Gorbachev
  was going to make a bold promise today at the United Nations.
The reporters even dared to say
  that the leader of the communist world
  was bringing a "Christmas surprise" to New York City.
This time, they were right.
A new burst of hope for peace came with Gorbachev's proposal
  of Soviet troop reduction for Europe.
In the midst of a war-weary world,
  there seems to be a step toward peace.

The hope of that first Christmas also came into a world of war.
When the young girl Mary walked the streets of Nazareth
  she saw Roman soldiers,
  a reminder to the Jews that they were not in charge of their destiny.
They were a people whose hopes were crushed.

This gospel of Luke for today's Feast of the Immaculate Conception
  comes out of a war tradition,
  a tradition of the Lord fighting for the people.
The angel, who announces the coming of the Savior,
  is called Gabriel,
  a name which reminds us that "God is strong."

Gabriel's message to Mary
  is the claim that God is powerfully at work
  for those who can't fight their own battles.

268

"You shall give him the name Jesus," he says.
"Jesus" means the one who saves people in time of trouble.

In our own day, the phrase "Just say no"
   has become a popular one,
   especially for young people who want to win a personal war on drugs.
This new war cry is a good one
   and has brought together legions of young warriors.
It's a cry that can be used not only in our battle with drugs,
   but with all the other battles we fight with the serpent
   who tries to convince us that we are missing something in life
   when we follow God's word.

But today's feast reminds us of another cry
   that we all need in our personal and global battles.
It's the cry of Mary
   who says in the midst of her confusion and fear,
     "Let it be done to me as you say."
Mary is totally open to God's word.
Mary agrees to play a vital part
   in the unfolding mystery of human salvation.

Mary reminds us that the peace of the reign of God will come about
   when we learn to listen to what God is saying to us
   and to our world.
Mary tells us that there is more to life than
   "Just say no."
Like her, we must listen to the angels in our lives
   and "Just say yes."